Nita Mehta's Punjabi Khaana

Nita Mehta
M.Sc. (Food & Nutrition), Gold Medalist

co author
HARVEEN CHOUDHRY

SNAB
Publishers Pvt. Ltd.

Nita Mehta's
PUNJABI KHAANA

© Copyright 2001-2002 **SNAB** Publishers Pvt Ltd

WORLD RIGHTS RESERVED: The contents - all recipes, photographs and drawings are original and copyrighted. No portion of this book shall be reproduced, stored in a retrieval system or transmitted by any means, electronic, mechanical, photocopying, recording or otherwise, without the written permission of the publishers.

While every precaution is taken in the preparation of this book, the publishers and the author assume no responsibility for errors or omissions. Neither is any liability assumed for damages resulting from the use of information contained herein.

TRADEMARKS ACKNOWLEDGED: Trademarks used, if any, are acknowledged as trademarks of their respective owners. These are used as reference only and no trademark infringement is intended upon.

Reprint 2002

ISBN 81-7869-007-1

Food Styling & Photography: **SNAB**

Layout and laser typesetting:

National Information
Technology Academy
3A/3, Asaf Ali Road
New Delhi-110002
☎ 3252948

Published by:

SNAB
Publishers Pvt Ltd
3A/3 Asaf Ali Road
New Delhi-110002

Editorial and Marketing office:
E-348, Greater Kailash-II, N.Delhi-48
Fax: 91-11-6235218 *Tel:* 91-11-6214011, 6238727
E-Mail: nitamehta@email.com
snab@snabindia.com

The Best of Cookery Books *Website:* http://www.nitamehta.com
Website: http://www.snabindia.com

Printed at:
THOMSON PRESS (INDIA) LIMITED

Distributed by:
THE VARIETY BOOK DEPOT
A.V.G. Bhavan, M 3 Con Circus
New Delhi - 110 001
Tel: 3327175, 3322567; Fax: 3714335

Price: Rs.189/-

Introduction

Punjab is a land of healthy, robust people. Punjabis believe in living life to the fullest. Their folk songs and Bhangra (folk dance) are well known all over. They have hearty appetites and enjoy good food. Infact, they give a lot of importance to food.

For most, the scope of Punjabi cuisine is limited to "Sarson ka Saag aur Makki di Roti" or "Dal Makhani" but there is more to the Land of Five Rivers. The Tandoori Murg and Curry culture is fast spreading all over the world. People in London and New-York etc. are getting acquainted with Indian food and Punjabi food appears to be a hot favourite. Beli Ram, who reigned supreme as the "King of Punjabi Cooking" may be no more, but the magic that he wove with his culinary skill lives on. His cooking has been brought alive in this book with "Meat Beli Ram" named in his honour.

Here is a book to help you prepare and enjoy Punjabi food as it is prepared in Punjabi households. All the recipes have been created using the simplest ingredients and techniques. Dairy products, leafy vegetables and grains have been used to infuse flavour, colour and aroma. Kashmiri red chilli powder (degi mirch) has been used in the recipes as it imparts a rich red colour without making the dish too hot. The recipes are simple and quick and yet extravagant and exotic!

Contents

Introduction 5

MAIN DISHES

CHICKEN 9

Murg Lahori 10
Surkh Kukkad 11
Nimbu Dhania Kukkad 12
Hariyali Murg 13
Chitta Kukkad (Safed Murg) 14
Dahi Murg 15
Murg Kali Mirch 16
Quick Makhani Murg 17
Makhani Murg 18

Khaja Murg 20
Murg Achaari 21
Kadhai Murg 22
Masala Murg 23
Khus Badaam Murg 24
Methi Murg 25
Dhania Aloo Murg 26
Murg Adraki 27
Kesar-illaichi Handi Murg 28

MUTTON 29

Meat Beli Ram 30
Kofta Curry 31
Dahiwala Mutton 32
Dum Ka Meat 33
Raarha Meat 34

Shalgam Wala Meat 35
Masaledar Mutton 36
Keema Matar 38
Mutton Waali Dal 39
Chaampe - Mutton Chops 40
Saag wala Mutton 41

FISH 42

Fried Fish 43
Nimbu Waali Machhi 44
Koliwada Fish 44
Tandoori Fish 45

Amritsari Machhi 46
Taya ji Di Machhi 48
Tomato Fish 49

VEGETABLES 50

Paneer Makhani 51
Dum Aloo 52
Punjabi Kadhi 53
Methi Aloo 54
Pindi Chhole 55
Gobhi Masala 56
Shimla Mirch Aloo Waali 58
Punjabi Rajmah Curry 59
Dal Makhani (Maanh Sabat) 60
Chitte Matar Tamatar 61
Paneer Tikka 62
Sukhi Maanh Di Dal 63
Saboot Gobhi 64
Paalak Paneer 65
Masala Bhindi Aloo 66
Punj Rattani Dal 68
Baingan Di Kachri 69
Gur Waale Shalgam 69
Lahori Malai Kofte 70
Bhein Masala 72
Tandoori Gobhi 73
Chholia Te Paneer 74
Matar Khumba Curry 75
Sarson Da Saag 76
Tawa Paneer Masala 78
Aloo Vadi 79
Khaja Aloo 80

ROTI & CHAAWAL 81

VEGETARIAN

Missi Roti 82
Tandoori Roti 82
Makki Di Roti 84
Methi Wali Makki Di Roti 84
Matar Vadi Wale Chaawal 85
Bhature 85
Gobi De Paranthe 89
Mooli De Paranthe 89
Poodina Parantha 91
Quick Peethi Poori 91
Amritsari Nan 92
Lachha Parantha 93

NON-VEGETARIAN

Khasta Keema Parantha 83
Keemae De Chaawal 86
Chicken Kali Mirch Pulao 88
Champae Waale Chaawal 90
Keema Nan 92

SNACKS 94

VEGETARIAN

Paneer Pakore (Special)   96
Punjabi Aloo Tikki   100
Haryali Paneer Tikka   101
Dahi Bhalle   102
Gobi Pakore (Special)   105
Amritsari Paneer   105

NON-VEGETARIAN

Reshmi Kababs   95
Chicken Tikka   98
Besan Di Murgi   99
Murg Haryali Kababs   101
Chicken Lollipops   103
Shami Kababs   104
Tandoori Chicken   106
Fish Tikka   108
Malai Kababs   109

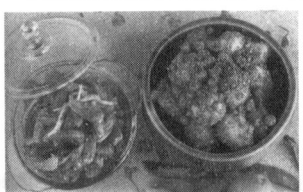

ACHAAR 110

VEGETARIAN

Sirke Waale Pyaaz   111
Khatti Arbi da Salaad   111
Gobi Shalgam Da Achaar   113
Kachalu Da Achaar   114
Amm Da Achaar   114

NON-VEGETARIAN

Khatta Mitha Kukkad Achaar   112
Mutton Achaar   115

DRINKS 116

Poodina Jeera Paani   118
Sardai   118

Punjabi Kanji   119
Lassi - Malai Maar Ke   119

MITHA 120

Suji Halwa   121
Pinni   121
Mithae Jauley   122
Badaam Te Gur De Laddu   122
Chhuare Te Chaawal Di Kheer   123

Pista Kesar Kulfi   123
Jalebi Te Rabri   124
Phirni   125
Kesar waale Mitthe Chaawal   126

Main Dishes
CHICKEN

Murg Lahori

Lahore was once a part of Punjab. This name has stuck on from the good old days and signifies a rich and a delicious white curry flavoured with kasoori methi.

Serves 5-6

1 chicken (800 gm) - cut into 12 pieces, (boneless chicken - cut into 2" pieces can also be used)
1 cup curd - hang for 15 minutes and beaten well till smooth
2 medium onions
6 flakes garlic
1" piece ginger
1-2 green chillies
10 tbsp oil
½ tsp garam masala
2 tsp salt
2 tsp white pepper (adjust to taste)
1½ tsp kasoori methi (dried fenugreek leaves)
150 ml (1 cup) fresh cream

1. Grind together onions, green chillies, garlic and ginger to a fine paste.
2. Heat oil. Add ground onions and fry on low heat for 3-4 minutes till pink and soft. Do not brown them.
3. Add chicken, salt, garam masala and white pepper. Fry for 3-4 minutes till chicken changes colour.
4. Add hung curd and kasoori methi. Mix well and stir for 3-4 minutes.
5. Cover, lower heat and cook till chicken is tender, approximately for 10 minutes.
6. Add fresh cream. Mix well and give one boil on low heat.
7. Serve hot garnished with kasoori methi.

Variation:

1. You can grill the chicken and then add it to the masala. There is no need to give much time for cooking the chicken if it is grilled. To grill chicken, spoon the chicken with some oil or just add 1-2 tbsp oil to the chicken kept in a bowl and mix. Grill in a moderately hot oven at 180°C for 10 minutes. Overturn and again brush the chicken with oil or pour a little oil on the chicken pieces with a spoon kept on the grill. Grill again for 5 minutes till tender and light brown.

Surkh Kukkad

A hot and bright red coloured, dry chicken.

Serves 5-6   Picture on page 1

1 chicken (800 gm) - cut into 12 pieces or pieces of your choice
1½ tsp garlic paste
1½ tsp ginger paste
2 large tomatoes - finely chopped
1½ tsp salt
1½ tsp dhania powder
1 tsp garam masala powder
6-7 tbsp oil/ghee

GRIND TOGETHER
20 dried, whole Kashmiri chillies - deseeded and soaked in water for ½ hour (see note given below)
2 medium sized onions

1. Break the stem of the red chillies and tap gently to remove all seeds. Soak in enough water to cover them. Keep aside for ½ hour. Drain the water from the chillies and grind them along with the onions to a smooth paste. Use a little water for grinding, if required.
2. Heat oil. Add ground red chilli-onion paste and ginger and garlic pastes. Fry well till the onion turns golden brown and leaves oil.
3. Add tomatoes and fry till they turn pulpy and get well mixed.
4. Add chicken, salt, dhania powder and garam masala. Mix. Stir fry for 3-4 minutes.
5. Lower the heat. Cover tightly and let it cook for 10-12 minutes or till chicken is tender. Sprinkle water in between if required.
6. Garnish with fresh coriander and lemon wedges and serve with hot chappaties.

Note: Kashmiri dry chillies impart a bright red colour to the chicken. These are much broader than the usual dry, red chillies. If you use the ordinary red chillies, reduce the quantity to 15 chillies.

Nimbu Dhania Kukkad

A dry chicken flavoured with lemon and coriander.

Serves 5-6

1 chicken (800 gms) - cut into 12 pieces or pieces of your choice (600 gm boneless can also be used)
6 flakes (large) garlic - crushed (1½ tsp)
2 tsp ginger - grated
6-8 tbsp oil
juice of 2-3 lemons (depending on your taste)
5-6 tbsp fresh coriander - chopped

SPICES
¼ tsp haldi powder
½ tsp jeera powder (cumin powder)
½ tsp dhania powder (coriander powder)
2 tsp salt, or to taste
½ tsp garam masala powder
1 tsp red chilli powder

1. Heat oil. Add chicken. Cook on high heat till the chicken gets nicely browned.
2. Remove chicken from oil and keep aside.
3. In the same oil add crushed garlic and grated ginger. Cook for 1 minute.
4. Add all the spices and mix well.
5. Add the browned chicken and mix well.
6. Add 3/4 cup water. Cover. Lower the heat and cook for 10 minutes or till chicken is tender.
7. Add lemon juice and fresh coriander. Mix well and serve.

Note: This chicken can be served as a snack. You can use boneless or only legs also. Make it absolutely dry if you want to serve it as a snack.

Hariyali Murg

Chicken pieces coated with a green paste.

Serves 4-5

CHICKEN
400 gms boneless chicken - cut into 1½" - 2" pieces
1½ tsp ginger paste, 1½ tsp garlic paste
6 tbsp curd, 3 tbsp flour (maida)
½ tsp salt

HARIYALI PASTE (GRIND TOGETHER)
1½ cups fresh dhania - chopped
1½ cups fresh spinach (paalak) - chopped
¼ cup fresh methi - chopped or 2 tbsp kasoori methi
4-5 flakes garlic, 1" piece ginger
1 large onion
2 green chillies (can increase according to taste)

OTHER INGREDIENTS
5 tbsp oil/ghee
1 tsp salt
1 tsp dhania powder
3/4 cup fresh cream
3/4 tsp garam masala powder
3-4 tbsp lemon juice (juice of 1 large lemon)

1. Mix all ingredients under chicken and marinate chicken in it for 1-2 hours in the fridge.
2. Brush the wire rack or tray of the oven with oil. Place chicken pieces on it. Brush chicken pieces with oil or dab them with oil using the fingers. Grill in a moderately hot oven at 180°C for 10 minutes. Overturn and again brush with oil. Grill again for 5 minutes till the chicken turns tender and light brown. Keep aside.
3. To prepare the gravy, mix paalak and methi together. Add ½ tsp salt and mix well. Leave for ½ hour. Wash well.
4. Grind together fresh dhania, paalak, methi, ginger, garlic, onion and green chillies to a fine paste.
5. Heat oil/ghee. Add hariyali paste. Fry for 2-3 minutes.
6. Add salt and dhania powder. Cook for 2 minutes.
7. Add cream and grilled chicken. Mix well. Check salt.
8. Just before serving, add garam masala and lemon juice. Mix well and serve garnished with tomato wedges.

Chitta Kukkad (Safed Murg)

A flavourful white masala chicken, prepared with exotic spices.

Serves 5-6

4 chicken breasts - each cut into 4 pieces (for boneless) or 800 gms chicken - cut into 12 pieces or of your choice
5 tbsp oil
½ cup milk
½ cup cream
fresh dhania for garnishing

GRIND TOGETHER
2 tbsp cashewnuts or blanched almonds
4-5 flakes garlic
1" piece ginger - chopped
1 green chilli - chopped
1½ cups curd

CRUSH TOGETHER - SPICES
2 blades of javetri (mace)
1 tsp saunf powder (fennel powder)
seeds of 3-4 chhoti illaichi - (green cardamom)

OTHER MASALAS & SPICES
¼ tsp grated jaiphal (nutmeg)
½ tsp jeera powder
½ tsp dhania powder
½ tsp garam masala powder
2 tsp salt, or to taste
½ tsp pepper powder, or to taste

1. Put cashews, garlic, ginger, green chilli and curd in a grinder and churn till smooth.
2. Heat oil. Add the curd-cashew mixture. Cook on high flame stirring all the time for 4-5 minutes.
3. Add chicken and cook on high flame till it changes its colour, for 4-5 minutes.
4. Reduce heat. Add the crushed spices and all the other masalas and spices. Mix well.
5. Add milk. Cover and cook for 15 minutes or till chicken gets tender and little masala remains.
6. Add cream. Mix and remove from fire. Garnish with fresh dhania and serve.

Dahi Murg

A delicious and fast recipe for a masala chicken. Once you taste it, you will want to have it again and again! The recipe requires very few ingredients.

Serves 5-6

1 chicken (800 gm) - cut into 12 pieces
6 tbsp oil/ghee
1½ tsp salt
1 tsp red chilli powder (adjust to taste)
1 cup curd - beat till smooth

GRIND TOGETHER TO A PASTE
1 large onion
3-4 flakes garlic
3/4" piece ginger

1. Grind together onion, garlic and ginger using a little water if needed to a fine paste.
2. Heat oil/ghee. Add ground paste and fry till it turns rich brown in colour.
3. Add salt and red chilli powder. Mix and add chicken. Stir fry till chicken changes colour, for about 3-4 minutes.
4. Beat the curd well and add to the chicken. Keep stirring continuously till it boils. This prevents the curd from curdling.
5. Lower heat, cover and cook till chicken is tender, for about 10-12 minutes.
6. Increase heat and cook till the required gravy remains. The gravy should be thick and usually once the chicken is tender, it requires no further cooking.
7. Garnish with fresh coriander and serve.

Note:

1. 2 sliced capsicums can be added towards the end (when the chicken is nearly cooked) to give the dish a different flavour.
2. 2 tsp kasoori methi can be added towards the end for added flavour.
3. Instead of red chilli powder, you may use black pepper powder and enjoy the difference it makes to the preparation.

Murg Kali Mirch

Delicious dry chicken - can be served as the main dish or a snack.

Serves 5-6

1 chicken (800 gm) - cut into 12 pieces
6-7 tbsp butter (preferably Amul)
2 tbsp grated ginger
1 tsp salt
1¼ tsp freshly ground pepper (grind it coarsely)
3-4 tbsp lemon juice (adjust to taste)

GARNISHING
some fresh coriander - chopped
3-4 saboot kali mirch (peppercorns) - crushed

1. Heat butter on medium flame. (If the heat is too much, the butter will burn). Add grated ginger. Fry on medium heat till slightly brown.
2. Add chicken, salt and pepper and fry till chicken changes colour, for about 4-5 minutes.
3. Lower heat, cover and let it cook for about 10-12 minutes or till chicken is tender.
4. Increase heat, add lemon juice and cook till dry.
5. To serve, heat chicken and spoon out on to the serving dish leaving the fat (melted butter) behind. Sprinkle coarsely pounded pepper and fresh coriander and serve.

Quick Makhani Murg

This is an adaptation of the original makhani murg that can be made fast but is equally delicious. A great favourite!

Serves 5-6

5 tbsp Amul butter
1 chicken (800 gms) - cut into 12 pieces or 600 gm boneless chicken
2 tsp garlic paste
2 tsp ginger paste
5 large tomatoes - pureed well in the mixer
½ cup ready made tomato puree
1½ tsp salt
1 tsp red chilli powder (adjust to taste)
2 tbsp kasoori methi (dried fenugreek leaves)
1 tsp garam masala powder
1 tsp sugar
1 cup milk
1 cup thin malai or thin cream (should be fresh)

1. Melt butter on low flame. Add chicken and fry on high heat for 4-5 minutes till it changes colour.
2. Add garlic and ginger paste. Fry for another 2-3 minutes.
3. Add fresh tomato puree.
4. Add ready made tomato puree, salt, red chilli powder, kasoori methi, garam masala and sugar. Give one boil. Lower heat and cook covered for 10 minutes or till the chicken turns tender.
5. Keeping the flame low, add milk, stirring continuously.
6. Add malai/cream. Give 1-2 boils, stirring all the time. Serve hot garnished with fresh coriander leaves.

Makhani Murg

Butter Chicken cooked the authentic way! This is probably the most popular Punjabi dish after tandoori chicken.

Picture on facing page *Serves 5-6*

1 tandoori chicken - cut into 12 pieces (see note below & recipe of tandoori chicken on page 106)

MAKHANI GRAVY
2 tbsp butter, 2-3 tbsp oil, 1 tej patta (bay leaf)
2 tbsp ginger-garlic paste
½ kg (6-7) tomatoes - blended to a very smooth puree
2-3 tbsp cashewnuts - soaked in hot water for 15 minutes, drained and ground to a very fine paste with a little water
¼ tsp Kashmiri or degi mirch or red chilli powder
1 cup milk, 2 tbsp cream
½ tsp garam masala, 1 tsp tandoori masala, ¼ tsp sugar or to taste
salt to taste

1. Prepare tandoori chicken as given on page 106. If you don't have a tandoor or an oven, see note given below to cook chicken in the kadhai.
2. To prepare the makhani gravy, heat butter and oil together in non stick pan. Add tej patta. Stir for a few seconds. Add ginger and garlic paste, cook until liquid evaporates and paste just changes colour.
3. Add pureed tomatoes, degi mirch and sugar. Cook until the puree turns very dry and fat separates. Add salt to taste.
4. Add cashew paste, stir for 2 minutes on medium heat. Remove from fire and cool for 15-20 minutes. Add milk and about ½ cup of water to get the desired gravy. Return to fire. Keeping on low heat, bring to a boil, stirring constantly.
5. Add chicken. Simmer for 2 minutes till the gravy turns to a bright colour. Remove from fire and stir in cream, stirring continuously. Add garam masala and tandoori masala. Stir. Remove from fire. Garnish with 1 tbsp of fresh cream, slit green chillies and coriander.

Note: To prepare tandoori chicken for butter chicken, if you do not have a tandoor or an oven, simply marinate the chicken as given on page 106 and cook in a non stick pan or kadhai instead of a tandoor. Add the marinated chicken pieces to 4-5 tbsp hot oil in a kadhai. Stir fry on high flame till the chicken is brown and crisp. Lower heat, cover and cook for 5 minutes till chicken is tender. Put it in makhani gravy.

Khaja Murg

A chicken curry with the richness of powdered cashews.

Serves 5-6

1 chicken (800 gm) - cut into 12 pieces
100 gms/14 tbsp kaju pieces - dry grind to a fine powder

GRIND TOGETHER TO A PASTE
2 large onions
1" piece ginger
1-2 green chillies
5-6 flakes garlic

OTHER INGREDIENTS
7-8 tbsp ghee/oil
1½ tsp red chilli powder
2 tsp salt, or to taste
1 tsp garam masala powder
4 tomatoes - pureed in the mixer
3/4 cup curd - well beaten
fresh coriander for garnishing

1. Grind kaju pieces dry to get a fine powder. Keep aside.
2. Grind together green chillies, onions, garlic and ginger to a fine paste.
3. Heat ghee/oil. Add ground onions and fry till golden brown.
4. Add salt, red chilli powder and garam masala. Mix well.
5. Add pureed tomatoes. Mix well. Cover, lower heat and let it cook for 10-12 minutes, or till oil separates.
6. Uncover and add chicken.
7. Increase heat and cook for 4-5 minutes till well fried. Add 1½ cups water. Mix well. Lower heat, cover and cook till chicken is tender for (8-10 minutes).
8. Reduce heat. Add well beaten curd. Keep stirring till it boils.
9. Add kaju powder. Mix well. Add enough water to get a thick curry. Give 3-4 boils. Remove from fire. Serve garnished with fresh coriander.

Murg Achaari

Serves 5-6 *Picture on back cover*

1 chicken (800 gm) - cut into 12 pieces
10 tbsp mustard oil
2 large onions - chopped finely or grated
2 tbsp ginger paste
2 tbsp garlic paste
1 tsp haldi powder
2 tsp salt
2 tsp sugar
2 tsp red chilli powder (Kashmiri)
1 cup curd - well beaten
4 tbsp lemon juice
some fresh dhania for garnishing

COLLECT TOGETHER
8-10 laung (cloves)
5-6 chhoti illaichi (green cardamoms)
1 tsp shah jeera (black cumin)
1 tsp methi dana (fenugreek seeds)
½ tsp kalaunji (onion seeds)
2 tsp rai (mustard seeds)
a pinch of hing (asafoetida)
5-6 whole, dry red chillies

1. Heat mustard oil till it smokes. Remove from fire and cool.
2. Heat oil again. Add all the collected spices - cloves, cardamoms, jeera, methi seeds, kalaunji, rai, hing and 5-6 whole, dry red chillies. Fry for ½ minute till methi dana turns golden.
3. Add onions and fry till golden brown.
4. Add ginger and garlic paste. Fry for 1-2 minutes.
5. Add chicken, salt, haldi, sugar and red chilli powder. Fry for 3-4 minutes on high flame.
6. Add well beaten curd. Keep stirring till it boils. Cook, stirring all the time for another 2 minutes.
7. Cover, lower heat and cook for 12-15 minutes or till chicken is tender.
8. Add lemon juice. Give 1-2 boils. Add ¼ cup water if you like and give 2-3 boils.
9. Serve hot, garnished with fresh dhania.

Note: Paneer or Dum aloo made in this way is also very delicious.

Kadhai Murg

Serves 4

A dry preparation of chicken, flavoured with fenugreek and coriander.

1 medium sized (800 gms) chicken - cut into 12 pieces
6-7 tbsp oil
½ tsp methi dana (fenugreek seeds)
3 whole, dry red chillies
3 large onions - cut into slices
15-20 flakes garlic - crushed & chopped, 1 tbsp ginger paste
4 large tomatoes - chopped, ¼ cup (4 tbsp) tomato puree
2 tsp salt, or to taste, ¼ tsp amchoor, ½ tsp garam masala, 1 tsp red chilli powder
1 tsp dhania powder (ground coriander)
1½ tbsp saboot dhania (coriander seeds) - roasted lightly on a tawa and coarsely pounded or crushed on a chakla-belan (rolling board & pin)
½ cup cream
½ cup chopped green coriander
1 capsicum - cut into thick fingers
2" piece ginger - cut into match sticks
1-2 green chillies - cut into thin long slices

1. Dry roast saboot dhania (coriander seeds) on a tawa lightly. Do not make them brown. Pound them on a chakla-belan (rolling board & pin) to split the seeds. Keep aside.
2. Heat oil in a kadhai. Reduce heat. Add methi dana and whole red chillies and stir for a few seconds.
3. Add onion and cook on medium heat till light brown.
4. Add garlic and stir for 1 minute.
5. Add tomatoes. Cook for 4-5 minutes. Add ginger paste.
6. Add the saboot dhania, red chilli powder and dhania powder.
7. Add chicken and bhuno for 7-8 minutes on high flame, stirring well to mix everything together.
8. Add salt, amchoor and garam masala. Cover and cook for 10-15 minutes till tender, stirring occasionally.
9. Add tomato puree and chopped green coriander. Cook for 1-2 minutes.
10. Add the capsicum, ginger match sticks and green chilli slices. Mix well.
11. Reduce heat. Add cream. Mix well for 2-3 minutes and remove from fire. Serve hot.

Masala Murg

Serves 5-6

1 chicken (800 gm) - cut into 12 pieces or of your choice

SOAK TOGETHER FOR 1-2 HOURS
2 tbsp khus-khus (poppy seeds) and 2 tbsp magaz (melon seeds) - soaked together in ½ cup warm water for 1-2 hours

GRIND TOGETHER
1 large onion
3-4 flakes garlic
1" piece ginger

OTHER INGREDIENTS
8 tbsp oil
1½ tsp salt
3 tsp Kashmiri red chillies (If using ordinary red chilli, decrease to 1-1½ tsp or according to taste)
1 tsp garam masala
3 large tomatoes - chopped fine or pureed in the mixer
5-6 tbsp curd - well beaten

1. Soak magaz and khus-khus in ½ cup water for 1-2 hours. Grind along with the water to a fine paste. Check that the khus is finely ground. Keep paste aside.
2. Grind onion, ginger and garlic also to a fine paste.
3. Heat oil and fry onion paste to a rich brown colour.
4. Reduce heat. Add salt, red chill powder, garam masala and pureed tomatoes. Mix well. Cover and cook on low heat for 12-15 minutes.
5. Uncover and increase the heat. Add chicken. Cook for 7-8 minutes or till oil separates.
6. Add ground khus-khus and magaz paste and again fry for 1-2 minutes on low heat.
7. Add beaten curd and mix well.
8. Lower heat, stir for 4-5 minutes or till oil separates.
9. Garnish with fresh coriander and lemon wedges and serve hot.

Note: To make chicken curry, after step 8 add 1½ cups water. Boil for a few minutes and then serve.

Khus-Badaam Murg

Chicken in whitish masala gravy.

Serves 5-6

1 chicken (1 kg) - cut into pieces of your choice
4 tbsp khus-khus (poppy seeds) - soaked in ½ cup warm water for 1-2 hours
15-20 almonds - soaked in water and skinned
8 tbsp ghee
5-6 laung (cloves)
12 saboot kali mirch (peppercorns)
1½ tsp salt, ½ tsp garam masala
1½ tsp pepper powder, preferably white pepper
1 cup curd - beat well

GARNISHING

green chillies and a few almonds - slivered (cut into thin long pieces) (cut into thin long pieces)

1. Soak khus-khus and almonds in ½ cup warm water for 1-2 hours. Pick up the almonds and skin them. Grind both together with water to a very fine paste.
2. Heat ghee. Add cloves and peppercorns. Fry for 1-2 minutes.
3. Add chicken and cook on high heat for 3-4 minutes, stirring all the time till chicken changes colour.
4. Add beaten curd and keep stirring till it boils. Fry well till ghee separates.
5. Add salt, pepper and ground khus-khus paste. Stir to mix well.
6. Add 1½ cups water to get a thick masala gravy. Give 2-3 boils. Cover and cook on low heat for about 7-8 minutes or till chicken is tender.
7. Add garam masala. Increase heat and cook till a slight gravy remains.
8. Garnish with green chillies and slivered (cut into thin long pieces) almonds and serve hot.

Methi Murg

Serves 5-6

1 chicken (800 gms) - cut into small pieces or use boneless pieces
4 cups finely chopped fresh methi leaves (fenugreek greens)
2 cups curd - well beaten
8-10 tbsp ghee/oil
2 large tomatoes - pureed in the mixer
2 tsp salt
1½ tsp garam masala

GRIND TOGETHER
2 large onions
3-4 green chillies (use according to taste)
1½" piece ginger
6-7 flakes garlic

TOPPING
3-4 tbsp ghee
½ tsp red chilli powder

1. Grind together onions, green chillies, garlic and ginger to a fine paste.
2. Heat oil/ghee. Add onion paste and fry the paste to a rich brown colour.
3. Add tomatoes, salt and garam masala. Cook till tomatoes turn dry and oil separates.
4. Add chicken and fry well for 5-6 minutes.
5. Add chopped methi and curd. Stir till it boils.
6. Cook till dry. The chicken will get tender during this time, check if the chicken is not completely cooked, cover and keep on low heat for a few minutes till chicken turns tender.
7. When the chicken turns dry and tender, transfer to a serving dish.
8. Heat 4 tbsp ghee. Add red chilli powder. Remove from fire. Pour over the hot chicken. Serve immediately.

Dhania Aloo Murg

A delicious dry chicken with a strong dhania (coriander) flavour, as both, dry and fresh dhania is used in it's preparation.

Picture on cover   Serves 5-6

1 chicken (800) - cut into 12 pieces
1 large potato - peeled and cut into 8 pieces
8 tbsp dhania powder
2 tsp ginger paste
2 tsp garlic paste
1¼ tsp salt, 1 tsp garam masala powder, 1¼ tsp red chilli powder
1 cup ready made tomato puree
½ cup dahi - beat well till smooth
6-7 tbsp oil/ghee
a pinch of sugar (adjust to taste)
1 cup chopped hara dhania (fresh coriander)

1. Heat oil/ghee in a kadhai. Reduce flame and add garlic and ginger paste. Fry till light brown.
2. Add dhania powder. Fry for 1 minute.
3. Add chicken, potato pieces, salt, red chilli powder and garam masala. Fry till chicken changes colour, for about 5 minutes.
4. Add tomato puree, well beaten dahi and ½ cup water and sugar. Mix well.
5. Lower heat, cover and let cook for 10 minutes or till chicken is tender and dry.
6. Add lots of fresh green coriander. Mix well and remove from fire. Serve.

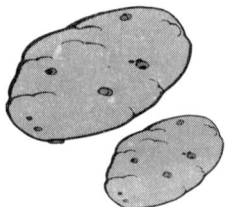

Murg Adraki

Chicken in ginger flavoured masala gravy.

Serves 5-6

1 chicken (800 gm) - cut into pieces of your choice (boneless chicken can also be used)
3 tbsp besan (gram flour) - dry roast in a kadhai
2 medium onions - ground to a paste or grated
1 tbsp ginger paste
1 tbsp finely chopped or grated ginger
3-4 saboot kali mirch (black peppercorns)
1 tej patta (bay leaves)
2 moti illaichi (black cardamoms)
2-3 laung (cloves)
1" piece dalchini (cinnamon)
7-8 tbsp oil
3 medium tomatoes - churned in the mixer to a puree
1½ tsp salt, or to taste
1½ tsp red chilli powder
½ tsp haldi powder
1 tsp garam masala powder
½ cup fresh cream
some ginger juliennes and fresh dhania for garnishing

1. Heat oil. Add laung, moti illaichi, dalchini, kali mirch and tej patta. Fry for 1 minute.
2. Add onion paste and fry till it turns brown.
3. Add ginger paste and chopped ginger. Fry for 1-2 minutes.
4. Add tomato puree, salt, red chilli powder, haldi and garam masala. Mix well. Cover, lower heat and let it cook for 10-15 minutes.
5. In the meanwhile, in another kadhai dry roast the besan. Keep stirring and roasting on medium heat till it turns light brown. Remove from fire and keep aside.
6. To the cooked tomato masala, add chicken and fry for 10-15 minutes. The chicken will get tender will frying, otherwise cover and cook on low heat till it gets tender.
7. Add roasted besan. Mix well.
8. Add cream and 1 cup water. Mix well. Give 1-2 boils on low heat.
9. Garnish with ginger juliennes and fresh dhania. Serve hot.

Kesar-illaichi Handi Murg

Serves 4

A thick chicken curry prepared with curd and cashewnut paste and flavoured with saffron and cardamoms.

1 medium size chicken (800 gm) - cut into 12 pieces
1 cup warm milk mixed with ¼ tsp kesar and seeds of 1 moti illaichi - crushed
5 tbsp oil
1 tej patta (bay leaf)
4 chhoti illaichi (green cardamoms)
10 cashewnuts - ground to a fine paste with little water
3 large onions - finely chopped
1 tbsp ginger paste
2 tbsp garlic paste
1 cup thick dahi (yogurt) - beaten well till smooth
1 tsp red chilli powder, salt to taste, ¼ tsp haldi
1 tsp garam masala powder
2 tbsp chopped coriander, to garnish

1. Grind cashewnuts to a very smooth paste with a little water.
2. Heat oil in a heavy bottomed handi or a pan. Add tej patta and broken green cardamoms. Stir for a few seconds.
3. Add the chopped onions and stir fry till light brown.
4. Add ginger-garlic paste and fry for 2-3 minutes, till water evaporates.
5. Add the chicken pieces and stir fry on high flame for about 5 minutes or till the chicken is half cooked and the water evaporates.
6. Mix cashewnut paste, chilli powder, salt, haldi and garam masala to the curd.
7. Add the curd mixture to the chicken, stir for a few minutes till the curd turns dry and blends well with the masala.
8. Add milk mixed with kesar and illaichi. Mix well.
9. Add ½ cup water. Seal the lid of the handi with atta dough and keep on low heat on dum for 15 minutes.
10. Garnish with fresh coriander leaves and serve with hot naan or roti.

Main Dishes
MUTTON

Meat Beli Ram

Beli Ram, who reigned supreme as the "King of Punjabi Cooking" may be no more, but the magic that he wove with his culinary skill lives on. His cooking has been brought alive with "Meat Beli Ram", a masala mutton, named in his honour.

Picture on page 1   Serves 6

1 kg lamb - clean chops and cut other parts into 1½" chunks

MARINADE
3 cups yogurt - beat till smooth
5 onions - cut into slices
4 tbsp finely chopped ginger
4 tbsp chopped garlic
10 chhoti illaichi (green cardamoms)
5 laung (cloves)
2 sticks dalchini (cinnamon)
2 tsp salt, or to taste
2 tsp Kashmiri deghi mirch

OTHER INGREDIENTS
3/4 cup ghee or oil
2 tbsp saboot dhania (coriander seeds) - crushed lightly on a chakla

1. Mix all the ingredients of the marinade together. Leave the lamb chunks in this marinade for 2 hours. Keep in the refrigerator.
2. Heat ghee in a pressure cooker.
3. Add coriander seeds and saute over medium heat until they begin to crackle.
4. Add the lamb, alongwith the marinade. Bring to a boil, stirring constantly.
5. Pressure cook to give 2 whistles. Reduce heat and keep on low heat for 20-25 minutes, or till mutton turns soft. Remove from fire.
6. When the pressure drops, bhuno the meat on medium heat until the fat leaves the masala and the mutton looks well fried. Adjust the seasoning.
7. Remove to a dish and serve with tandoori roti.

Kofta Curry

Serves 10-12

400 gms keema - wash and squeeze out all the water and grind well in the mixer
1" piece ginger - chopped
4 flakes garlic - chopped
1 egg
1 tsp red chilli powder (Kashmiri), 1½ tsp salt, 1 tsp garam masala

GRAVY
4 medium onions
1½" piece ginger, 6 flakes garlic
5-6 moti illaichi (black cardamoms), 2 tej patta (bay leaves)
1½" dalchini (cinnamon), 5-6 laung (cloves)
2 tsp red chilli powder (Kashmiri), 2 tsp salt, ½ tsp haldi
1 tsp dhania powder, 1 tsp jeera powder, 1 tsp garam masala
4 tomatoes - pureed in the mixer (1 cup)
12 tbsp curd
7 tbsp oil plus 3 tbsp pure ghee or 10 tbsp oil

1. Wash keema well and squeeze out all the water by placing it in a strainer and pressing it.
2. Grind the keema along with ginger and garlic to a fine paste.
3. Remove from mixer. Add egg, salt, garam masala and red chilli powder. Mix well. Form balls and keep aside.
4. For the gravy, grind together onions, ginger and garlic to a fine paste.
5. Heat oil and ghee. Add khada garam masalas - moti illaichi, dalchini, laung and tej patta and fry for 1 minute.
6. Add ground onions and fry well till it turns dark brown.
7. Add pureed tomatoes. Mix and add masalas - red chilli, salt, haldi, dhania, jeera and garam masala. Cook till tomatoes turn dry.
8. Add well beaten curd and keep stirring till oil separates.
9. Add 3 cups of water. Give a boil.
10. To the boiling gravy, one by one add the keema balls. Do not stir. Give 2-3 boils.
11. Lower heat. Cover and let them cook for 25-30 minutes or till the koftas turn soft. Garnish with fresh dhania and serve.

Note: For egg curry, instead of keema koftas, add full boiled eggs. They should be added towards the end and the amount of water reduced to 1½ cups. Let the gravy simmer for 15 minutes before adding eggs. Simmer for another 5-7 minutes and serve.

Dahiwala Mutton

A quick but delicious dish with very little gravy - which can be dried completely also. Champae (ribs) can also be prepared in this manner and can be served as a snack.

Serves 2-3

MARINATE FOR 1-2 HOURS
250 gms mutton
1 cup curd
3/4 tsp salt
3/4 tsp red chilli powder (Kashmiri)
3/4 tsp dhania powder

OTHER INGREDIENTS
5 tbsp oil/ghee
1 big onion - chopped (1 cup)
1 tsp garlic paste
1 tsp ginger paste

GARNISHING
¼ tsp garam masala and some kasoori methi

1. Mix together curd, salt, dhania powder & red chilli. Marinate mutton in this for 1-2 hours.
2. Heat oil/ghee in a cooker. Add chopped onions, ginger and garlic paste. Fry for 1-2 minutes.
3. Add mutton pieces without any extra marinade and fry for 5-7 minutes.
4. Add all the left over marinade. Mix well.
5. Add 1 cup water. Close the cooker and give 2-3 whistles. Keep on low heat for 30 minutes.
6. When pressure drops, add garam masala and kasoori methi. Mix well. Cook for 2-3 minutes, mixing all the time so that the onion gets minced and the masala gravy coats the mutton.
7. At the time of serving, heat ½-1 tbsp pure ghee. Add ¼ tsp red chilli powder. Cook for 1-2 seconds. Pour over hot mutton and serve.

Note: If you want a dry mutton, you can dry all the gravy.

Dum Ka Meat

Quick and delicious masala mutton. Requires no frying & no elaborate cooking. Definitely worth a try.

Serves 4

400 gms mutton (preferably without too many bones and no fat)
1 large onion - chopped
1 large tomato - chopped
4 tbsp pure ghee
3 tbsp mustard oil
1 cup curd - well beaten
2-3 flakes garlic - crushed to a paste
½ tsp ginger paste
2 chhoti illaichi (green cardamoms)
1 moti illaichi (black cardamom)
2-3 laung (cloves)
4-5 saboot kali mirch (peppercorns)
1" piece dalchini (cinnamon)
1 tej patta (bay leaf)
1¼ tsp salt
1¼ tsp red chilli powder
½ tsp garam masala

1. Mix everything together in the pressure cooker. There is no need to heat oil etc.
2. Close the cooker and give 2 whistles. Keep on low heat for 25 minutes. Remove from fire.
3. When the pressure drops, open the cooker. Check for tenderness. (If required pressure cook for a few more minutes).
4. Return to fire and cook for about 5 minutes, till a thick masala remains and the mutton looks well fried. Garnish with fresh dhania and serve.

Note: Potatoes or chicken can also be made this way. Give only 2 whistles and cut potatoes into large pieces, each potato cut into two or four pieces.

Raarha Meat

The name basically indicates a mutton dish that has been well fried.

Serves 2-3

250 gms mutton
3/4 cup curd - beaten well till smooth
1 tsp salt
5 tbsp ghee/oil
2 moti illaichi (black cardamoms)
1" stick dalchini (cinnamon)
1 tej patta (bay leaf)
1 big onion - finely chopped (1 cup)
1 tsp ginger paste
1 tsp garlic paste
1 big tomato - finely chopped (1 cup)
1 tsp red chilli powder, ½ tsp haldi powder
3/4 tsp garam masala powder

GARNISHING
some fresh chopped dhania leaves

1. Whisk curd. Add salt and mutton and let it marinate for 1-1½ hours.
2. Heat ghee/oil in a pressure cooker.
3. Add dalchini, illaichi and tej patta. Fry for few seconds.
4. Add onion. Fry till light brown.
5. Add ginger and garlic paste, haldi, garam masala and tomatoes. Cook till tomatoes are soft and well mixed.
6. Add mutton along with the marinade and cook till oil separates.
7. Add 3/4 cup water. Mix well. Close the cooker and give 1-2 whistles. Keep on low heat for 25 minutes. Remove from fire.
8. When pressure drops, open cooker and again fry till oil/ghee separates. Sprinkle fresh dhania on top and serve hot with rotis.

Shalgam Wala Meat

Serves 2-3

250 gms mutton
125 gms (2 medium) shalgam (turnips) - peeled and cut into 3/4" pieces
3 tbsp oil plus 2 tbsp pure ghee
2-3 laung (cloves)
1 large onion - sliced (1 cup)
½" ginger - chopped
2 cloves garlic - chopped
3-4 whole red chillies - deseeded and broken into small pieces
½ tsp dhania powder
1¼ tsp salt
½ tsp garam masala
½ tsp haldi
½ tsp red chilli powder (kashmiri)
1 cup curd - well beaten

1. Peel shalgam and cut into ½" - ¾" pieces.
2. In a pressure cooker, heat oil and ghee. Add laung and fry for 1 minute.
3. Add sliced onion, chopped ginger, garlic and broken red chillies. Fry till onion turns soft.
4. Add mutton, dhania powder, salt, garam masala powder, haldi, red chillies. Stir fry for 8-10 minutes on high heat.
5. Add ¾ cup water. Mix well and give one whistle in the cooker. Keep on low heat for 25 minutes to cook the mutton properly.
6. When the pressure drops, open and stir well. Keep stirring for sometime till all the onion gets mashed and well mixed.
7. Add shalgum and well beaten curd. Keep on fire and keep stirring till it boils. Close the cooker and give 2 whistles.
8. Open and serve hot, garnished with fresh dhania.

Note: Instead of shalgum, potatoes can also be used.

Masaledar Mutton

Picture on facing page   Serves 2-3

300 gms mutton
2 large onions - cut into rings
2 tbsp oil plus 3 tbsp pure ghee
1 tej patta (bay leaf)
1 tbsp garlic paste
1 tbsp ginger paste
3/4 tsp salt
3/4 tsp red chilli powder
3/4 garam masala
½ tsp haldi powder
3/4 tsp dhania powder
3/4 tsp jeera powder
2 large tomatoes - pureed in the mixer

GARNISHING
green chillies and ginger strips

1. In a pressure cooker heat oil and ghee. Add tej patta and onion rings. Fry till transparent.
2. Add ginger and garlic paste. Fry for 1 minute.
3. Add mutton and all seasonings. Fry for 8-10 minutes till oil separates and it has a well fried look.
4. Add fresh tomato puree. Mix well.
5. Add 3/4 cup water. Mix well and close the cooker.
6. Give 2 whistles. Keep on low heat for 25 minutes. The time will depend on the quality of the mutton.
7. Open the cooker after the pressure drops and cook till nearly dry.
8. Garnish with green chillies and ginger strips and serve with hot chappatis or paranthas.

Keema Matar

A very popular dish made regularly in most Punjabi homes.

Serves 2-3

5-6 tbsp oil/ghee
250 gms keema (mutton mince) - washed and drained well
3/4 cup shelled peas
4-5 laung (cloves)
1" dalchini (cinnamon)
4-5 saboot kali mirch (peppercorns)
1 large onion - chopped (1 cup)
5-6 flakes garlic - chopped fine
½" piece ginger - chopped fine
1 large tomato - chopped (1 cup)
1 tsp salt
3/4 tsp red chilli powder (adjust to taste)
3/4 tsp garam masala powder
½ tsp haldi powder

1. Heat oil/ghee in a pressure cooker. Add cloves, cinnamon and peppercorns. Fry for 1 minute.
2. Add chopped onions, ginger and garlic. Fry till onions turn rich brown in colour.
3. Add tomatoes, all seasonings and keema. Fry very well till oil separates.
4. Add peas. Mix well. Add 3/4 cup water. Close the cooker and give 3 whistles.
5. Open the cooker when pressure drops. Cook and dry as much as you like (some people like it absolutely dry and some like it wettish).
6. Garnish with fresh coriander and lemon wedges and serve.

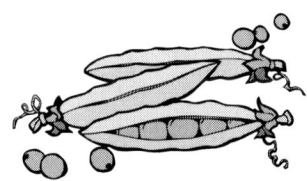

Mutton Waali Dal

Serves 2-3

250 gms mutton
1 cup channa dal
6 tbsp oil plus 2 tbsp pure ghee
2-3 laung (cloves)
3/4" dalchini (cinnamon)
2 medium onions - chopped
3 flakes garlic - chopped fine
3/4" piece ginger - chopped fine
2 tomatoes - chopped
1½ tsp salt
3/4 tsp garam masala
¼ tsp haldi
1¼ tsp Kashmiri red chilli powder (degi mirch)
2 tbsp lemon juice
fresh coriander for garnishing

1. In a pressure cooker heat oil and ghee. Add laung and dalchini.
2. Add chopped onions, ginger and garlic. Fry till onions turn soft.
3. Add mutton and fry for 4-5 minutes.
4. Add tomatoes, salt, garam masala, haldi and red chilli powder. Fry for 5-7 minutes.
5. Add washed channa dal. Fry for 2-3 minutes.
6. Add 6 cups water. Close the cooker. After 1 whistle lower heat and let it cook for about 20 minutes.
7. When the pressure drops, open, add lemon juice and mix well. (The dal should remain whole and should not become a paste).
8. Serve hot garnished with fresh dhania.

Champae - Mutton Chops

Serves 5-6

½ kg mutton (lamb) ribs
2 tsp garlic paste
1 tsp ginger paste
juice of 1 lemon
½ tsp salt, or to taste
½ tsp pepper, or to taste
5-6 tbsp oil

1. Wash mutton chops. Drain and pat dry on a kitchen towel.
2. Pound only the meat on the chops, hitting carefully with a rolling pin (belan), taking care not to hit on the bones, to flatten and break the tissue to make it tender. (you can make the butcher do it for you).
3. Rub salt, pepper, lemon juice, ginger and garlic paste on the chops. Keep the marinated chops aside for 2-3 hours or in the refrigerator if there is more time to serve.
4. Heat 5-6 tbsp oil in a pressure pan for shallow frying.
5. Add the chops. Cook on medium flame, stirring all the time. Cook until the water of the mutton dries.
6. Add 1½ cups water and give 2 whistles. Keep on low flame for 20 minutes, or till tender. Remove from fire.
7. After the pressure drops, if there is any excess water, dry it on fire and bhuno the chops. Serve hot with lemon wedges and onion rings.

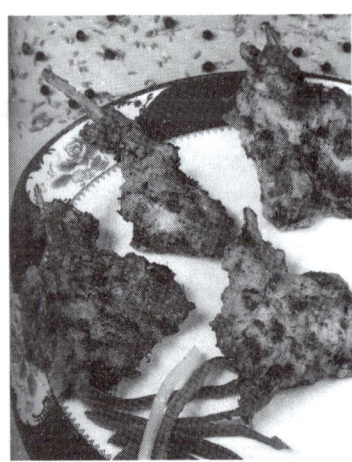

Saag wala Mutton

Picture on page 47 *Serves 2-3*

300 gms mutton
6 cups paalak (spinach) - washed and chopped very fine
garlic water (1 tsp crushed garlic soaked in 3-4 tbsp water)
1 moti illaichi (black cardamom)
2" stick dalchini (cinnamon)
4-5 laung (cloves)
2 medium onions - chopped fine (2 cups)
1 tsp garlic paste
1 tsp salt
½ tsp garam masala powder
3-4 green chillies - chopped
2 medium (1½ cups) tomatoes - chopped
5-6 tbsp oil

TOPPING
1-2 tbsp pure ghee
¼ tsp red chilli powder
some ginger juliennes (thin strips of ginger)

1. Heat oil in a pressure cooker.
2. Add moti illaichi, laung and dalchini. Fry for 1-2 minutes.
3. Add onions and fry till transparent.
4. Add garlic paste and mutton. Fry well for 4-5 minutes.
5. Add salt, garam masala, green chillies (chillies can be adjusted to taste) and tomatoes. Stir fry till tomatoes get soft and mix well with the mutton.
6. Add ½ cup water. Close the cooker and give 2 whistles. Keep on low heat for 20 minutes. Remove from fire.
7. When the pressure drops, open the cooker and add spinach/paalak and garlic water. Keep cooking till the water dries up and the mutton is tender. Transfer to a serving dish.
8. Heat ghee. Switch off gas. Add red chilli powder to hot ghee and immediately pour over the hot mutton.
9. Garnish with ginger strips and serve hot with tandoori roti or nan.

Note: Chicken saag wala can also be made this way. The chicken will not require any whistles in the cooker as it cooks fast. After frying with tomatoes lower heat, cover and cook till tender.

Main Dishes
FISH

Fried Fish

Punjabis love and enjoy fried and heavy food. Fried fish is a great favourite of the Punjabis and is made in many different ways. It is an excellent snack and is also served with the main meal.

Serves 4

600 gms fish (8 pieces) - preferably boneless and skinless

GRIND TO A PASTE
7-8 flakes garlic
5-6 green chillies
1" piece ginger
1 cup chopped fresh coriander leaves
4-5 tbsp lemon juice
2 tsp salt

COATING
6 tbsp maida (flour)
½ tsp salt
½ tsp red chilli powder
1 egg - beaten lightly
oil for frying

1. Rub fish with a little salt and lemon juice or besan. Wash well and pat dry.
2. Grind together garlic, chillies and ginger, chopped coriander, lemon juice and salt to a paste.
3. Rub the paste well on the fish. Leave the fish to marinate for 2-3 hours in the refrigerator.
4. Mix maida with salt and red chilli powder. Lightly beat the egg.
5. Heat oil for frying. Coat fish pieces with maida, dip in beaten egg and fry to a golden brown colour.
6. Serve hot with mint chutney or tomato sauce.

Note:

1. If fish is fried in mustard oil it has a better flavour and taste.
2. Large prawns can also be cooked in this way.

Nimbu Waali Machhi

A simple but delicious fish with the prominent flavour of pepper and lemon. Can be served as a snack.

Serves 2-3

400 gms fish (5-6 pieces) - preferably boneless and skinless
6 tbsp lemon juice
1½ tsp salt
3 tsp pepper - preferably freshly ground
2 tsp garlic paste, 2 tsp ginger paste
some cornflour for rolling (coating)
oil for frying

1. Rub fish with some salt and 1 tbsp lemon juice. Wash well to remove any smell.
2. Mix together 6 tbsp lemon juice, 1½ tsp salt, 3 tsp freshly ground pepper, ginger and garlic paste. Rub this on the fish and let it marinate for 2-3 hours in the fridge.
3. Heat oil. Roll each piece of fish in dry cornflour so that the cornflour coats the fish lightly. Deep fry till cooked and crisp. Serve hot with chutney/sauce garnished with lemon wedges.

Koliwada Fish

Serves 3-4

500 gms fish - cut into 2-3" pieces
1½ tsp garlic paste, 1½ tsp ginger paste
1½ tsp salt
2-2½ tsp red chilli powder (Kashmiri) - according to taste
1½ tsp amchoor, 1 tsp garam masala powder
½ tsp ajwain (optional), a pinch of orange red colour
1 tbsp maida
oil for frying

1. Rub fish with some salt. Wash well and squeeze out all the water.
2. In a bowl mix all ingredient together.
3. Add fish and mix well. Let it marinate for 1-2 hours.
4. Heat oil and deep fry the fish.
5. Serve hot with mint chutney. Garnish with lemon wedges and onion slices.

Note: Chicken and prawns can also be prepared in this manner.

Tandoori Fish

Delicious, succulent fish. Can be served as snack or with the main meal.
Serves 3-4

500 gms fish - cut into 5-6 pieces, preferably boneless and skinless
some melted butter or oil for basting
½ tsp shah jeera (black cumin)

MARINADE
2½ tsp Kashmiri red chilli powder (degi mirch)
1¼ tsp salt
½ tsp garam masala powder
1½ tsp amchoor
1 tsp dhania powder
1 tsp ginger paste
1 tsp garlic paste
3 tbsp lemon juice
¼ tsp shah jeera (black cumin)
½ tsp chaat masala

1. Rub fish with little salt and lemon juice. Wash and pat dry.
2. Mix all ingredients given under marinade.
3. Rub the marinade well all over the fish pieces and let it marinate for 2-3 hours.
4. Heat an oven at 180°C. Grease the wire rack and place fish pieces on it. Let it grill for 8-10 minutes.
5. Baste with melted butter/oil. Sprinkle ¼ tsp shah jeera and overturn basting and sprinkling rest of the shah jeera on the other side too.
6. Grill again for 8-10 minutes till well cooked and crisp. The time of grilling will depend on the thickness of the fish and may vary a little.
7. Sprinkle chaat masala and serve hot with mint chutney.

Note:

1. A small fish (pomfret) can be made whole in this way.
2. While grilling, always place fish pieces (or a whole fish) on a rack with the drip tray below it as it will leave some liquid which will drip down. If the fish is placed on a tray/thali the water will remain around the fish and hence make it soggy and it will not get crisp.

Amritsari Machhi

Delicious fried fish with the flavour of ajwain. Makes an excellent snack.

Serves 5-6

800 gms fish (10-12 pieces), preferably boneless and generally Sole fish is used but any fish can be used
2 tbsp plus 6 tbsp besan
some chaat masala for sprinkling on top
oil for frying

MARINADE
3 tsp ajwain
3 tsp garlic paste
3 tsp ginger paste
2½ tsp salt
3 tsp red chilli powder
2 tsp garam masala
8-10 tbsp lemon juice

1. Rub fish with a 1 tsp salt and 2 tbsp besan. Wash well to remove all smell.
2. Mix together all ingredients of the marinade.
3. Rub this marinade on the fish and leave the fish to marinate for 2-3 hours in the fridge.
4. At the time of serving, sprinkle 6 tbsp besan on fish and rub it so that the besan lightly coats the fish.
5. Deep fry to a golden brown colour till the fish is cooked and crisp.
6. Sprinkle chaat masala and serve hot garnished with onion rings, lemon wedges and sprigs of coriander or mint.

Note:

1. A few drops of colour (orange red) can be added to the marinade for a different colour.
2. For a different flavour 1-1½ tsp kasoori methi (dry fenugreek leaves) can be added in the marinade.

Saag Wala Mutton : Recipe on page 41 ➤

Taya ji Di Machhi

One of my uncle makes this fish. It is delicious and in our family it is called uncle's fish. This can be served as a snack or with the main meal.

Serves 4-5

400 gms fish (Singhara or any other fish of your choice) - preferably boneless and skinless, cut into medium size pieces
mustard oil for frying
fresh coriander leaves and lemon wedges for garnishing

MIX TOGETHER
2 eggs - beaten lightly
2 tbsp fresh coriander leaves - finely chopped
2 tsp garlic paste
1¼ tsp salt
1½ tsp Kashmiri red chilli powder (adjust to taste)
½ tsp dhania powder
½ tsp amchoor powder (increase to 1 tsp if you prefer a sour taste)
½ tsp garam masala

1. Rub fish pieces with salt and lemon juice well and wash. Pat dry.
2. Beat eggs lightly. Add fresh coriander, garlic paste, salt, red chilli powder, dhania powder, amchoor powder and garam masala powder. Mix well.
3. Add fish pieces and mix well so that fish is well coated with the mixture. Leave to marinate for 2-3 hours in the fridge.
4. Heat mustard oil. Pick up the fish pieces, leaving the extra marinade behind. Fry to a golden colour. Keep fish aside.
5. Heat a non stick frying pan. Add 1-2 tbsp mustard oil and swirl it around so that the bottom of the pan is coated with the oil.
6. Add fried fish pieces to the pan and pour all the remaining marinade on the fish. Cover and cook on low heat for 5-6 minutes, overturning the pieces once or twice to ensure even heating.
7. Serve hot garnished with fresh coriander leaves and lemon wedges.

Tomato Fish

Serves 4-5

500 gms fish - cut into 2"- 3" pieces (preferably boneless and skinless)
oil for frying

MARINADE
1 tsp salt
1 tsp red chilli powder
2 tbsp lemon juice
1 tsp dhania powder
1 tsp jeera powder

GRAVY
500 gms (6 medium) ripe red tomatoes - blanched (put in hot water and skin removed) and then pureed till smooth
5-6 tbsp oil
1 tbsp garlic paste
1¼-1½ tsp red chilli powder (kashmiri) - according to taste
1¼ tsp salt
1 tsp garam masala
1 tsp dhania powder
1½ tsp sugar
2 tbsp kasoori methi

1. Rub fish with a little salt and wash well to remove any smell.
2. Mix all ingredients given under marinade and marinate the fish in it for 10-15 minutes.
3. Heat oil and fry the fish lightly, a few pieces at a time. Do not make it crisp. Remove and keep aside.
4. Blanch tomatoes by boiling whole tomatoes in water for 4-5 minutes. Remove skin and puree them in a mixer to a smooth puree.
5. Heat oil. Add garlic and fry till light brown.
6. Add tomato puree and all other seasonings including kasoori methi. Give one boil, stirring continuously.
7. Slide in the fish pieces and let them boil for 4-5 minutes.
8. Serve hot garnished with fresh dhania and green chillies.

Main Dishes
VEGETABLES

Paneer Makhani

Serves 4

250 gm paneer - cut into 1" cubes
3 tbsp desi ghee or butter
½ tsp jeera (cumin seeds)
4-5 flakes garlic - crushed
1 tbsp kasoori methi (dried fenugreek leaves)
1 tsp tomato ketchup
½ tsp garam masala, 2 tsp dhania powder
1 tsp salt, or to taste, ½ tsp red chilli powder
½ cup water
½ cup milk
½ cup cream (optional)

GRIND TOGETHER
4-5 large (400 gm) tomatoes
2 green chillies
1" piece ginger

1. Grind together tomatoes, green chillies and ginger to a smooth puree.
2. Melt ghee or butter in a kadhai. Reduce heat. Add jeera. When it turns golden, add garlic.
3. When garlic starts to change colour add the tomato puree and cook till absolutely dry.
4. Add kasoori methi and tomato ketchup.
5. Add masalas - dhania powder, garam masala, salt and red chilli powder. Mix well for a few seconds. Cook till oil separates.
6. Add water. Boil. Simmer on low heat for 4-5 minutes. Reduce heat.
7. Mash 2-3 cubes of paneer and add to the gravy. Add the paneer cubes.
8. Keep aside to cool till serving time.
9. At serving time, add enough milk to the cold paneer masala to get a thick curry, mix gently. (Remember to add milk only after the masala turns cold, to prevent the milk from curdling. After adding milk, heat curry on low heat.)
10. Heat on low heat, stirring continuously till just about to boil.
11. Add cream, keeping the heat very low and stirring continuously. Remove from fire immediately. Serve with paranthas.

Dum Aloo

Serves 8

6 regular or 16 baby potatoes (chhote aloo)
2 tbsp cashewnut pieces - soaked in 3 tbsp curd for 15 minutes and ground to a paste
6 tbsp oil
2 moti illaichi (black cardamoms), 1 dalchini (cinnamon)
2 onions - chopped roughly
2" piece ginger - chopped
3 tomatoes
1 green chilli
¼ tsp haldi
½ tsp dhania powder
3/4 tsp red chilli powder
3/4 tsp garam masala
2 tsp salt, or to taste
2-3 tbsp freshly chopped coriander

1. Peel potatoes. Prick them all over with a fork. Cut into 4 pieces if regular ones or leave whole if baby potatoes are available. Soak in salted water for 15 minutes.
2. Drain and wipe dry potatoes. Deep fry potatoes on medium flame till golden brown and till they feel soft when a knife is inserted in them. Remove from oil only when well cooked. Keep aside.
3. Soak kaju in dahi for 15 minutes. Grind together to a fine paste.
4. Grind the onions and ginger to a paste. Keep onion paste aside.
5. Grind the tomatoes and green chilli to a fine paste.
6. Heat 6 tbsp oil. Add moti illaichi and dalchini. Wait for a minute and add the onion paste. Stir for 5-7 minutes on low flame, till oil separates and onions turn golden brown.
7. Add haldi, dhania powder, red chilli powder, garam masala and salt. Cook on low heat till onions get well browned.
8. Add the freshly pureed tomatoes. Cook till dry and oil separates.
9. Add dahi-kaju paste. Cook for 4-5 minutes till oil separates. Add enough water (about 2½ cups) to get a thick gravy. Boil.
10. Add fried potatoes. Simmer on low heat for 5-7 minutes till potatoes are well coated with masala. Add chopped coriander and serve.

Punjabi Kadhi

Serves 4-6

1 cup besan (gram flour)
2 cups khatti dahi (sour curd)
½ tsp haldi powder, 2½ tsp salt or to taste
¾ tsp red chilli powder (according to taste)
2 tbsp oil
½ tsp jeera, ½ tsp methi daana (fenugreek seeds)
1 moti illaichi (black cardamoms), 2 laung (cloves)
3-4 dry, red chillies

PAKORE (DUMPLINGS)
1 cup besan (gram flour), 1/3 cup water- approx.
1 big onion - chopped finely, 1 small potato - chopped finely
½" piece ginger - chopped finely, 2 green chillies - chopped finely
½ tsp red chilli powder, 1 tsp salt, ½ tsp garam masala, 1 tsp dhania powder
a pinch of baking powder, oil for frying

TADKA/TEMPERING
2 tbsp oil, ½ tsp jeera (cumin seeds), ¼ tsp red chilli powder, preferably red chilli flakes

1. Mix curd, besan, salt, haldi, red chilli powder and 5 ½ cups water. Beat well till smooth and no lumps remain.
2. In a big heavy-bottomed pan, heat oil. Add jeera, methi daana, moti illaichi and laung. Add whole, red chillies too.
3. When jeera turns golden, add curd-water mixture. Stir continuously till it boils. After one good boil, lower heat and simmer for 15 minutes, stirring occasionally. Remove from fire and keep aside.
4. To prepare pakoras, mix besan with water to make a thick paste. Beat well. Add all other ingredients given under pakoras. Beat well to get a soft dropping batter.
5. Heat oil and drop spoonfulls of batter. Deep fry pakoras on medium heat till golden brown.
6. Add pakoras to the ready kadhi.
7. At serving time transfer the hot kadhi to a serving dish.
8. For the tadka, heat oil in small pan. Reduce flame and add jeera.
9. When it turns golden, remove from fire and red chilli powder. Pour oil on to the hot kadhi in the dish. Serve hot with boiled rice.

Note: To get red chilli flakes, dry grind whole red chillies in a small spice grinder coarsely.

Methi Aloo

Serves 4

200 gm chhote aloo (baby potatoes) - washed and scrubbed well or 3 medium potatoes - cut into 1" cubes
1 large bunch (500 gm) methi
4 tbsp mustard oil (sarson ka tel), preferably, or any other cooking oil
3-4 flakes garlic - crushed
½ tsp garam masala
¼ tsp amchoor
½ tsp red chilli powder
½ tsp haldi
1½ tsp salt, or to taste

1. Remove the hard stem of methi and chop leaves finely. Rub 1 tsp salt on them and keep aside for 15 minutes.
2. Wash and scrub small potatoes. Do not peel. If small potatoes are not available, peel and cut 3 medium potatoes into 1" cubes.
3. Wash methi in several changes of water. Strain. Squeeze well to remove excess water.
4. Heat mustard oil to smoking point. Remove from fire. Heat oil again. Reduce flame.
5. Add garlic. When it changes colour, add potatoes. Bhuno for 5 minutes.
6. Add methi also. Mix.
7. Add haldi, salt, amchoor, garam masala and red chilli powder. Mix well. Cook covered for 12-15 minutes, till potatoes get cooked.
8. Uncover and bhuno methi for 10 minutes. Serve hot with chappatis.

Pindi Chhole

Serves 4 *Picture on page 2*

PRESSURE COOK TOGETHER
1 cup channa kabuli (Bengal gram)
2 tbsp channe ki dal (split gram)
2 moti illaichi (big cardamoms)
1" stick dalchini (cinnamon)
2 tsp tea leaves - tied in a muslin cloth or 2 tea bags
¼ tsp soda-bicarb

MASALA
2 onions - chopped finely
1½ tsp anaardana (pomegranate seeds) powder
1 big tomato - chopped finely
1" piece ginger - chopped finely
1 green chilli - chopped finely
½ tsp garam masala
1 tsp dhania powder
1 tsp channa masala powder
salt & red chilli powder to taste

1. Soak channa & channe ki dal overnight or for 6-8 hours in a pressure cooker. Next morning, discard water. Wash channas with fresh water and add moti illaichi, dalchini, tea leaves, ¼ tsp soda and enough water to cover the channas nicely.
2. Pressure cook all the ingredients together to give one whistle. After the first whistle, keep on low flame for about 20 minutes. Keep aside.
3. Heat 4 tbsp oil. Add onions. Saute till transparent. Add anaardana powder. Cook stirring till onions turn dark brown. (Do not burn them).
4. Add chopped tomatoes, ginger and green chill. Stir fry for 3-4 minutes.
5. Add dhania powder, chilli powder and garam masala. Mash and stir fry tomatoes occasionally till they turn brownish in colour and oil separates.
6. Strain channas, reserving the liquid. Remove tea bags from the boiled channas and add to the onion-tomato masala. Mix well. Add salt. Stir fry gently for 5-7 minutes.
7. Add channa masala and salt. Add the channa liquid. Cook for 15-20 minutes on medium heat till the liquid dries up a little.
8. Serve, garnished with onion rings, green chillies and tomato wedges.

Gobhi Masala

Fried cauliflower, served with capsicum and tomato chunks in yogurt masala.

Picture on facing page   *Serves 4*

1 medium cauliflower - cut into medium size florets with a little stalk
1 tsp jeera (cumin seeds)
2 onions - chopped
1½ tbsp ginger-garlic paste
2- 4 green chillies - deseeded & chopped
¼ tsp garam masala
¼ tsp red chilli powder, 1 tsp salt or to taste
2 tsp kasoori methi (dry fenugreek leaves)
½ cup dahi (yoghurt) - beat till smooth
1 tomato - cut into 8 big pieces
1 large capsicum - cut into 1" cubes

1. Break the cauliflower into medium florets, keeping the stalk intact.
2. Heat oil in a kadhai for deep frying. Add all the cauliflower pieces and fry to a light brown colour. Remove from oil and keep aside.
3. Heat 2 tbsp oil on a tawa. Add jeera. When it turns golden, add chopped onions. Stir till transparent.
4. Add the ginger-garlic paste, green chillies, salt, chilli powder, garam masala, kasoori methi and curd. Stir-fry for 2-3 minutes till the curd dries up a little.
5. Add capsicum and tomato cubes. Fry for 1-2 minutes.
6. Add cauliflower and mix well on low heat for 2 minutes till the vegetables get well blended with the masala. Serve hot.

Gobhi Masala; Tawa Paneer Masala: Recipe on page 78 ➤

Shimla Mirch Aloo Waali

Serves 6

(250 gm) 4 shimla mirch (capsicums) - deseeded and cut into fingers
2 medium potatoes - cut into fingers
4 tbsp oil
1 tsp jeera (cumin seeds)
2 large onions - cut into slices
1" piece ginger - chopped finely
1 tsp dhania powder
½ tsp garam masala
¼ tsp haldi
1 tsp salt, or to taste
½ tsp red chilli powder
¼ tsp amchoor
2 tomatoes - chopped
1 tomato - cut into 4 long slices and pulp removed

1. Peel potatoes. Cut into 4 long pieces. Cut each piece into 2-3 fingers.
2. Heat oil. Add jeera. Reduce flame.
3. When jeera turn golden, add onions. Cook till light brown.
4. Add finely chopped ginger. Stir for a few seconds.
5. Add masalas - salt, dhania powder, garam masala, haldi, red chilli powder and amchoor. Mix well for a minute.
6. Add chopped tomatoes and cook for 2-3 minutes.
7. Add potatoes. Stir fry for 1-2 minutes. Cover and cook till potatoes are done and feel soft when a knife is inserted in them.
8. Add 2 tbsp water.
9. Add capsicum. Cook uncovered, stirring occasionally, for 10 minutes or till capsicum turn slightly soft but still crisp. Sprinkle some salt on the capsicum slices, if required.
10. Add the tomato cut into long strips. Mix well and do not cook further.
11. Remove from fire and serve hot with chappatis.

Punjabi Rajmah Curry

Servings 6

1½ cups lal rajmah (red kidney beans) - soaked overnight
1 tbsp channe ki dal (split gram) - soaked overnight
2½ tsp salt or to taste
2 onions
6-8 flakes garlic, 1" piece ginger
6 tbsp oil
1 tej patta (bay leaf)
2 laung (cloves)
1 moti illaichi (black cardamom)
3 tomatoes - pureed in a blender
½ cup curd - beaten well
¼ tsp haldi, 3 tsp dhania powder, ¼ tsp amchoor
½ tsp garam masala, 1 tsp chilli powder, or to taste
2 tbsp chopped coriander

1. Pressure cook rajmah, channe ki dal with salt together with about 10 cups water to give one whistle. Keep on low flame for 20 minutes. Remove from fire.
2. Grind onion, ginger and garlic to a paste.
3. Heat 5 tbsp oil in a heavy bottomed kadhai. Add tej patta, moti illaichi and laung. Wait for 1 minute.
4. Add onion paste and stir fry till golden brown.
5. Reduce heat. Add haldi, dhania powder, amchoor, garam masala and red chilli powder. Stir for a few seconds.
6. Add tomatoes pureed in a blender. Cook till tomatoes turn dry and oil separates.
7. Add beaten curd and stir continuously on low flame till the masala turns red again and oil separates.
8. Strain and add the rajmahs, keeping the water aside. Stir fry on low flame for 2-3 minutes, mashing occasionally.
9. Add the water of the rajmahs and pressure cook again for 8-10 minutes on low flame after the first whistle.
10. Remove from fire. Add freshly chopped coriander leaves. Serve hot with chappatis or boiled rice.

Dal Makhani *(Maanh Sabat)*

Picture on cover   Serves 6

1 cup urad saboot (whole black beans)
2 tbsp channe ki dal (split gram dal)
2 tbsp rajmah (kidney beans) - soaked for at least 6 hours or overnight, optional
1 tbsp ghee or oil
5 cups of water, 1 ½ tsp salt
2 dry whole red chillies, preferably Kashmiri red chillies
1" piece ginger
4 flakes garlic (optional)
4 tomatoes - pureed in a grinder
1 tbsp kasoori methi (dry fenugreek leaves)
3 tbsp ghee or oil
2 tsp dhania (coriander) powder
½ tsp garam masala
2 tbsp butter
¼ cup fresh malai, beaten well and mixed with ¼ cup milk to make it ½ cup

1. Clean, wash dals. If you want to add rajmah, soak both dals and rajmah together in a pressure cooker for 6 hours or overnight.
2. Grind ginger and garlic together to a paste.
3. Discard water from the soaked dals and add 6 cups of fresh water.
4. Pressure cook both dals and rajmah with 1 tbsp ghee, salt, half of the ginger-garlic paste and the dry, red chillies. Keep the left over paste aside.
5. After the first whistle, keep on low flame for 40 minutes. Remove from fire. After the pressure drops, mash the hot dal a little. Keep aside.
6. Heat ghee. Add tomatoes pureed in a grinder. Cook until thick & dry.
7. Add the left over ginger-garlic paste, garam masala and coriander powder. Cook until ghee separates.
8. Add kasoori methi. Cook further for 1-2 minutes.
9. Add this tomato mixture to the boiled dal.
10. Add butter. Simmer on low flame for 20-25 minutes, stirring and mashing the dal occasionally with a kadchhi against the sides of the cooker.
11. Add beaten malai mixed with milk. Mix very well with a kadcchi. Simmer for 15-20 minutes more, to get the right colour and smoothness. Remove from fire. Serve hot.

Note: Originally the dal was cooked by leaving it overnight on the burning coal angithis. The longer the dal simmered, the better it tasted.

Chitte Matar Tamatar

Peas with tomatoes in a rich white gravy.

Serves 4 *Picture on page 67*

1 cup boiled or frozen peas
1 small firm tomato - cut into 4 pieces
2 tbsp cashewnuts - soaked in ¼ cup hot water for 5 minutes
3/4 cup dahi
seeds of 2 chhoti illaichi (green cardamoms)
3 tbsp oil
½ tsp jeera (cumin seeds)
2 tsp kasoori methi
2 onions and 1" piece ginger - ground to a paste
1 tsp dhania powder
½ tsp garam masala
½ tsp red chilli powder
¼ tsp sugar
1 tsp salt or to taste
½ cup milk
1 tsp tandoori masala

1. Drain cashewnuts and grind along with curd and seeds of chhoti illaichi to a fine paste.
2. Heat 3 tbsp oil. Add jeera. Wait till it turns golden.
3. Add onion and ginger paste. Stir fry on low flame till light brown. Reduce flame.
4. Add kasoori methi, dhania powder, garam masala, red chilli, sugar & salt. Stir for ½ minute.
5. Gradually add curd-cashewnut mixture, a little at a time, stirring continuously. Bhuno for 4-5 minutes till masala turns thick and oil separates.
6. Add milk and 1 cup water. Boil. Simmer for 5-7 minutes, on low flame till gravy turns thick.
7. Add boiled peas. Mix.
8. Add tomato pieces and tandoori masala. Give 2-3 boils and serve hot.

Paneer Tikka

Serves 4

300 gm paneer - cut into 1½" squares of 1" thickness
1 large capsicum - deseeded and cut into 1" pieces (12 pieces)
1 onion - cut into 4 pieces and then separated

MARINADE
¼ cup drained thick dahi (yogurt) - (hang ½ cup yogurt for 15 minutes)
2 tbsp thick malai or thick cream
a few drops of orange colour or a pinch of haldi (turmeric)
2 tbsp oil
1 tbsp (level) maida
½ tsp amchoor
½ tsp kala namak, 3/4 tsp salt, or to taste
1 tbsp tandoori masala

GRIND TOGETHER
1" piece ginger, 5-6 flakes garlic
2 dried, whole red chillies - soaked in water for 10 minutes and drained

1. Drain soaked red chillies. Grind ginger, garlic and red chillies to a paste.
2. To the ginger-garlic-chilli paste, add hung dahi, malai, 2 tbsp oil, 1 tbsp maida, amchoor, salt, kala namak, tandoori masala and colour or haldi.
3. Brush a grill rack of the oven or skewers generously with oil.
4. Dip each paneer piece in the marinade and toss well to coat all sides. Arrange paneer on a greased wire rack of the oven or on the skewers. After all the paneer pieces are done, put the capsicum and onions - both together in the left over marinade and mix well to coat the vegetables with the marinade. Leave the vegetables in the bowl itself.
5. At the time of serving, put the paneer pieces placed on the wire rack in the hot oven at about 200°C. Grill till almost done, for about 15 minutes. Grill the paneer till it gets dry and starts getting crisp. Sprinkle some oil on the paneer pieces. Now remove the vegetables from the bowl and put them also in the oven on the sides of the paneer. Grill everything together for another 5 minutes. The vegetables should not be grilled for too long.
6. Remove from the oven. Serve immediately (really hot), sprinkled with some lemon juice and chaat masala.

Sukhi Maanh Di Dal

Serves 4

PRESSURE COOK TOGETHER
1 cup urad dhuli dal (split black beans) - soaked for ½ hour and drained
½" piece ginger - very finely chopped
2 green chillies - very finely chopped
½ tsp haldi
1¼ tsp salt
1 cup water

TADKA/TEMPERING
4 tbsp desi ghee or oil
1 big onion - finely chopped
1" piece ginger - cut into match sticks
1 big tomato - finely chopped
½ tsp chilli powder
½ tsp garam masala
¼ tsp amchoor
2 tbsp chopped coriander leaves to garnish

1. Clean, wash dal. Soak dal in water for ½ hour. Strain dal.
2. Pressure cook dal with 1 cup water and all the other ingredients. When the first whistle comes, reduce heat and keep on low flame for 1 minute only.
3. Remove from fire. Open the cooker only after the pressure drops down. Keep aside.
4. At the time of serving, heat ghee. Add onions. Cook till light brown.
5. Add ginger match sticks and stir for a few seconds till onions turn brown.
6. Add tomatoes. Cook for 2-3 minutes.
7. Add ½ tsp chilli powder, ½ tsp garam masala and ¼ tsp amchoor. Cook for ½ minute.
8. Pour the hot oil or ghee over the hot dal. Mix gently.
9. Serve hot sprinkled with chopped coriander.

Saboot Gobhi

Serves 4

Whole cauliflower, cooked and topped with

2 very small whole cauliflowers
4 tbsp oil

MASALA
3 onions - sliced finely
3 tomatoes - roughly chopped, 1" ginger - chopped
2 tbsp curd
½ tsp gram masala, ½ tsp red chilli powder, ½ tsp amchoor, salt to taste
¼ cup boiled peas - to garnish

1. Remove stem of cauliflower. Boil 5-6 cups water with 2 tsp salt. Put the whole cauliflower in it and leave it in hot water for 10 minutes. Remove from water and wash. Wipe dry with a towel.
2. Heat 5-6 tbsp oil in a large flat kadhai. Put both cauliflowers with flower side down in oil. Cover and cook on medium flame, stirring occasionally till the cauliflower turns golden and gets cooked. Remove from oil.
3. To prepare masala, grind onions to a paste.
4. Heat ½ tbsp oil in a clean kadhai. Add the chopped tomatoes and ginger. Cook for 4-5 minutes till they turn soft. Grind the cooked tomatoes to a paste.
5. Heat 3 tbsp oil in a kadahi. Add the onion paste, cook till onions turn brown.
6. Add tomato paste. Cook for 3-4 minutes on low flame till masala turns dry.
7. Add well beaten curd. Cook till masala turns reddish again.
8. Add red chilli powder, amchoor, garam masala and salt. Cook for 1 minute.
9. Add 2-3 tbsp water to get a thick, dry masala. Boil. Cook for 1 minute on low flame. Remove from fire.
10. Insert a little masala in between the florets of the fried cauliflower, especially from the backside.
11. To serve, arrange the cauliflowers on a platter. Add 3-4 tbsp water to the masala to make it a masala gravy. Boil. Pour over the arranged cauliflowers. Heat in a microwave or a preheated oven.

OR

Heat the cauliflower in a kadhai in 1 tbsp oil at the time of serving. Heat the masala separately by adding 2-3 tbsp water to get a thick masala gravy. Arrange the heated cauliflowers on a serving platter. Pour the hot masala gravy over it.

12. Sprinkle some boiled peas on it and on the sides. Serve.

Paalak Paneer

Serves 4 *Picture on page 67*

200 gm paneer - cut into 8 big pieces and deep fried to reddish brown
500 gm paalak (spinach) - chopped (5 cups)
3-4 green chillies - chopped
2 big onions - ground to a paste
6 tbsp ready-made tomato puree (Godrej's puree)
2" piece ginger - crushed to a paste (2 tsp)
10-12 flakes garlic (optional) - crushed to a paste (2 tsp)
4 tbsp desi ghee or oil
½ tsp haldi powder, 1 tsp garam masala, 1 tsp salt, or to taste

TADKA
1-2 tbsp ghee or oil
1" piece ginger - finely chopped
1-2 green chillies - cut into 2 pieces
1 tsp red chilli powder

1. Discard stems of palak leaves. Wash leaves in lots of water to remove grains of sand or soil.
2. Pressure cook with ¼ cup water to give one whistle. Keep on low flame for 5 minutes. Remove from fire. Cool.
3. Grind cooked paalak along with green chillies in a mixer to a coarse paste.
4. Heat ghee and fry onions to a golden colour.
5. Add tomato puree and cook on low flame for 2 minutes.
6. Add ginger and garlic paste. Cook for ½ minute.
7. Add salt, haldi and garam masala. Stir for 1 minute.
8. Add paalak and cook for 1 minute.
9. Add 2 cups hot water to make it thinner. Boil. Keep on low flame for 10-15 minutes. Remove from fire and transfer to a serving dish.
10. At serving time, heat ghee for tadka. Add ginger. Cook on low heat till it turns golden. Remove from fire and add green chillies. Mix. Add red chilli powder and immediately pour over the hot palak. Serve.

Masala Bhindi Aloo

Picture on facing page   Serves 4

300 gm small sized bhindi (lady's finger)
2 potatoes - cut into thin fingers
3-4 flakes garlic - crushed roughly
2 tbsp ready made tomato puree
1 tsp kasoori methi (dry fenugreek leaves)
1½ tsp dhania powder
½ tsp garam masala
3/4 tsp salt
½ tsp red chilli powder
¼ tsp sugar
oil to fry

1. Wash bhindi. Wipe with a clean kitchen towel. Cut the tip of the head of each bhindi.
2. Heat oil for frying in a kadhai to medium hot temperature. Add half of the bhindi and fry on medium flame for about 5 minutes till it gets cooked. Remove from oil.
3. Fry the second batch of bhindi also.
4. Fry the potato fingers to a golden brown colour on medium flame till they get cooked and turn golden.
5. Remove all the oil from the kadhai. Heat 2 tbsp oil again in the kadhai.
6. Reduce flame. Add garlic and fry till it changes colour. Remove from fire.
7. Add tomato puree, kasoori methi, 1½ tsp dhania powder, ½ tsp garam masala, 3/4 tsp salt, ½ tsp red chilli powder and ¼ tsp sugar.
8. Return to fire. Stir for 1-2 minutes on low flame.
9. Add the fried potatoes. Mix. Add the bhindi. Stir for a few minutes. Cover and cook on low flame for 3-4 minutes. Serve.

Masala Bhindi Aloo ; Matar Tamatar in Cashew Gravy: Recipe on page 61 ➤
Paalak Paneer: Recipe on page 65 ➤

Punj Rattani Dal

A combination of five lentils are used to prepare this dal delicacy.

Serves 4

FIVE DALS

(WASH ALL DALS AND SOAK TOGETHER FOR 2 HOURS)
¼ cup saboot moong dal (green)
¼ cup saboot masoor dal (brown)
¼ cup saboot urad dal (black)
¼ cup channa dal (yellow)
¼ cup tur dal (yellow)

OTHER INGREDIENTS
2 tbsp ghee
1 tsp shah jeera (black cumin seeds)
½ onion - chopped
2 tsp coriander powder, ½ tsp red chilli powder
½ tsp haldi, 1½ tsp salt, or to taste

TEMPERING
4 tbsp white butter
1 tomato - chopped finely
½ cup yoghurt - beat well till smooth
½ tsp garam masala
seeds of 1 moti illaichi - crushed on a chakla
½ tsp red chilli powder
¼ cup coriander - chopped

1. Heat ghee in a heavy bottomed pan. Add shah jeera and saute over medium heat until they begin to crackle.
2. Add onion, saute until light brown.
3. Drain the dals and add to the onion. Bhuno for 4-5 minutes on low heat.
4. Add about 5 cups water and bring to a boil. Reduce heat and remove scum.
5. Add coriander powder, red chilli, haldi and salt, cover and simmer for about ½ hour, until lentils are done.
6. To prepare the tempering, melt butter in a kadhai, add tomatoes, yoghurt and garam masala, bhuno over medium heat until the fat leaves the sides. Add crushed seeds of moti illaichi. Stir for a few seconds. Add red chilli powder.
7. Add the cooked lentils and stir for 3-4 minutes. Remove to a bowl, garnish with coriander and serve hot.

Baingan Di Kachri

Crisp brinjal slices coated with wheat flour.

Serves 4

1 medium round baingan (brinjal) - washed & cut into thin slices (15 slices)
1 tsp kuti laal mirch (red chilli flakes)
4-5 tbsp atta (whole wheat flour)
3-4 tbsp oil for shallow frying

1. Sprinkle 1½ tsp salt on baingan ke slices, leave to sweat for 15-20 minutes. Drain out water. Pat dry.
2. Spread them on a plate. Sprinkle red chilli flakes and some atta on the slices. Overturn the slices and sprinkle more red chilli flakes and atta on the other side too. Keep aside till serving time.
3. At the time of serving, heat 3-4 tbsp oil in a frying pan or a tawa.
4. Fry 4-5 baingan slices at a time till crisp on both sides. Turn with the help of a chimta (tongs) or a knife to brown both sides.

Gur Waale Shalgam

A sweet and tangy vegetable.

Serves 2-3

½ kg shalgam (turnips)
1½ tsp gur (powdered) or shakkar
3 tbsp oil
1" piece ginger - grated, 1 green chilli - chopped
2 tbsp chopped coriander
1 tsp dhania powder, ½ tsp red chilli powder
½ tsp garam masala, ½ tsp salt, or to taste

1. Peel the shalgams and cut into 1" cubes (like potatoes).
2. Put in a pressure cooker with ½ cup water and give 2 whistles. Remove from fire.
3. Heat oil. Add ginger and green chillies. Let ginger turn light brown.
4. Add shalgam. Cook mashing occasionally till the water dries and it looks like a halwah.
5. Add gur and masalas. Mix well for 2-3 minutes. Add coriander & serve.

Lahori Malai Kofte

Serves 6

150 gms paneer (cottage cheese) - grated
2 small boiled potatoes - grated
2 tbsp maida
½ tsp garam masala
½ tsp red chilli powder, 3/4 tsp salt, or to taste
2-3 tbsp maida (plain flour) - to coat

FILLING
½ onion - very finely chopped
½" tsp piece ginger - very finely chopped
4-5 kajus (cashews) - chopped
¼ tsp each of salt, red chilli powder, garam masala

GRAVY
a few strands kesar (saffron)
3 big onions
1½" piece ginger
2 dry, red chillies
2 tej patta (bay leaf)
4-5 chhoti illaichi (green cardamoms)
4 tbsp kaju (cashewnuts) - powdered
½ cup fresh thin malai - beaten with a fork or churned in the mixi for a second
3 tbsp desi ghee
½ tsp garam masala, 3/4 tsp red chilli powder, 1½ tsp salt, or to taste
1 tbsp kasoori methi
1½ cups milk mixed with 2 cups water

1. To prepare the koftas, mix grated paneer, potatoes, red chilli powder, salt, garam masala and 2 tbsp maida.
2. Mix well till the mixture is smooth. Make 12 balls.
3. For the filling, heat 2 tsp ghee. Add onions and ginger. Fry till golden brown. Add kaju, salt, garam masala and chilli powder. Remove from fire.
4. Flatten each ball of paneer mixture, put 1 tsp of onion filling in each ball. Form a ball again. Roll each ball in maida. Dust to remove excess maida.
5. Deep fry 1- 2 koftas at a time in medium hot oil. Keep aside.
6. To prepare the gravy, soak kesar in 1 tbsp warm water.
7. Grind onions, ginger & dry red chilli to a fine paste. Heat 2 tbsp ghee in a heavy

contd...

bottomed kadhai and add the onion paste.
8. Add tej patta and chhoti illaichi. Cook on low flame for about 10-15 minutes till onions turn light brown and ghee separates.
9. Add masalas - garam masala, red chilli powder and salt.
10. Add malai. Cook for 3-4 minutes till masala turns brown again.
11. Add kaju powder. Cook for ½ minute.
12. Add milk mixed with water, to make a gravy. Boil. Simmer on low flame for 5 minutes.
13. Add kasoori methi. Discard bay leaves from the gravy.
14. Add kesar, keeping aside a little for garnishing.
15. To serve, boil gravy. Add koftas. Keep on low heat for ½ a minute. Serve immediately, sprinkled with cream and dotted with soaked kesar.

Bhein Masala

Serves 4

300 gm (2 medium) bhein or kamal kakri (lotus stem), thick ones
4 tbsp oil
2 tbsp atta (whole wheat flour)

FILLING (MIX TOGETHER)
2" piece ginger - crushed to a paste
8-10 flakes garlic - crushed to a paste
1 tsp salt
½ tsp red chilli powder
½ tsp haldi
½ tsp amchoor
1½ tsp dhania powder
3/4 tsp garam masala
1 tsp oil

1. Peel bhein. Cut into 1½" long pieces.
2. Put bhein in a pressure cooker with 1 cup water and ½ tsp salt. Keep on fire to give 1 whistle and then reduce heat and keep for 7-8 minutes on low heat. Remove from fire and keep aside.
3. Mix all ingredients of the filling together. Make a slit in each boiled piece of bhein and fill the stuffing with the knife as you keep making the slit. Fill all the pieces and keep the left over filling aside.
4. Heat 4 tbsp oil in a large kadhai. Add 2 tbsp atta. Bhuno for 2 minutes on low heat.
5. Add the left over ginger-garlic filling and bhuno for a few seconds.
6. Add the bhein and stir fry for 5-7 minutes on medium flame till well browned. While bhuno-ing the bhein, spread out the vegetable in the kadhai so that all the pieces get well browned and turn crisp. Do not collect the vegetable in the centre of the kadhai and do not overlap them.
7. Add fresh coriander and mix well. Serve hot with paranthas.

Tandoori Gobhi

Whole cauliflower grilled to perfection in a tandoor or an oven.

Serves 4-6

1 medium size cauliflower - with 1-2" stalk & washed well

MARINADE
¾ cup thick curd - hang for ½ hour
¼ cup cream or malai
1 tbsp oil
2 tbsp besan (gram flour)
½ tbsp ginger paste
2 tsp tandoori masala
4-6 saboot kali mirch (black peppercorns) - crushed
½ tsp red chilli powder, ¼ tsp haldi
1 tsp salt

TO SERVE
2 onions - cut into fine rings
2 tbsp finely chopped coriander
½ tsp chaat masala
1 tomato - cut into slices

1. Boil 4 cups water with 1 tsp salt.
2. Add cauliflower. When the water starts to boil again, remove from fire. Let the cauliflower be in hot water for 3-4 minutes. Remove from water and keep aside.
3. Wipe the cauliflower with a clean kitchen towel. Keep aside.
4. Mix together in a bowl all ingredients of the marinade. Insert the marinade inside the cauliflower florets, from the top and the bottom also. Rub the top with the left over marinade. Keep aside for atleast 1 hour.
5. Brush the grilling rack of the oven generously with oil. Place the marinated cauliflower on the greased grilling rack.
6. Grill in a hot oven at 200°C for 30 minutes or more till brown specs appear on the cauliflower. Keep aside till serving time.
7. To serve, cut the whole cauliflower into 4 pieces right through the stalk. Cut each piece further into 2 pieces. Sprinkle chaat masala.
8. Add fresh coriander and chat masala to the onions.
9. To serve, heat gobhi in an oven or microwave till really hot. Arrange the pieces neatly in serving platter. Heat in an oven or microwave. Sprinkle lemon juice. Garnish with prepared onion rings, tomato slices, lemon wedges and mint sprigs.

Chholia Te Paneer

Every winter, the Punjabi housewife spends half the morning shelling fresh Bengal gram to use it in various dishes like rice, parantha or with meat. Here it is used in combination with paneer to make a delicious curry.

Serves 4

200 gm chholia (fresh green gram)
100 gms paneer (cottage cheese) - cut into 1" cubes & deep fried
4-5 tbsp oil
2 moti illaichi (black cardamoms), 2 laung (cloves)
1" stick dalchini (cinnamon)
3 onions - grind to a paste
1" piece ginger, 4-6 flakes garlic - crushed to a rough paste
3 tomatoes - pureed
½ tsp haldi, ¼ tsp amchoor
3/4 tsp red chilli powder
2 tsp dhania powder
3/4 tsp garam masala
1½ tsp salt, or to taste
2 tbsp chopped coriander
1 tsp tandoori masala

1. Deep fry big paneer pieces to a nice reddish brown colour. Keep aside.
2. To prepare gravy, grind onions to a paste in a grinder. Grind tomatoes separately.
3. Crush ginger and garlic to a rough paste.
4. Heat oil in a kadhai. Add 2 moti illaichi (black cardamom), 2 laung (cloves), 1" stick dalchini (cinnamon). Wait for a minute.
5. Add onion paste. Fry onion paste in oil till light brown.
6. Add crushed ginger and garlic.
7. Add haldi, amchoor, red chilli powder, dhania powder, garam masala and salt. Cook on low flame till onions turn brown.
8. Add tomato puree. Cook till dry. Bhuno the masala for about 7-8 minutes on low flame. Bhuno till oil separates.
9. Add chholia. Bhuno for 5-7 minutes. Add 2½ cups water.
10. Transfer the vegetable to a pressure cooker. Add fried paneer.
11. Close the pressure cooker and give one whistle. Keep on low flame for 2 minutes. Remove from fire.
12. After the pressure drops, add tandoori masala. Mix well.
13. Serve garnished with chopped coriander.

Matar Khumba Curry

Serves 6-8 *Picture on page 97*

1 packet (200 gm) mushrooms (khumba) - trim stalks & cut into 4 pieces
1 cup peas (shelled)
4 tbsp oil
2 moti illaichi (black cardamoms), 2 laung (cloves)
2 tsp salt, or to taste
2 tsp dhania powder
¼ tsp each - red chilli powder, garam masala, haldi

GRIND TOGETHER TO A PUREE
3 tomatoes
1 green chilli

GRIND TOGETHER TO A PASTE
1 large onion
6-8 flakes garlic
1" piece ginger

1. Heat oil. Add moti illaichi and laung. Wait for 1 minute.
2. Add onion-garlic-ginger paste. Cook stirring continuously light till brown. Remove from fire.
3. Add masalas - salt, dhania powder, red chilli powder, garam masala and haldi.
4. Return to low heat and cook for a few seconds. Add 1 tbsp water.
5. Add the tomato-green chilli puree. Cook till dry and oil separates.
6. Add mushrooms and peas. Stir fry for 5 minutes. Add 1-2 tbsp water if required.
7. Add 2 cups water. Cook on low medium heat for about 15 minutes till peas turn soft and oil separates.
8. Serve curry with rice or chappatis.

Sarson Da Saag

Picture on facing page   Serves 6

1 bundle (1 kg) sarson (mustard greens)
250 gm spinach or baathoo
2 shalgam (turnips) - peeled and chopped, optional
3-4 flakes garlic - finely chopped, optional
2" piece ginger - finely chopped
1 green chilli - chopped
3/4 tsp salt, or to taste
2 tbsp makki ka atta (maize flour)
1½ tsp powdered gur (jaggery)

TADKA/TEMPERING
3 tbsp desi ghee
2 green chillies - finely chopped
1" piece ginger - finely chopped
½ tsp red chilli powder

1. Wash and clean mustard leaves. First remove the leaves and then peel the stems, starting from the lower end and chop them finely. (Peel stems the way you string green beans). The addition of stems to the saag makes it tastier but it is important to peel the stems from the lower ends. The upper tender portion may just be chopped. Chop the spinach or baathoo leaves and mix with sarson.
2. Put chopped greens with ½ cup water in a pan.
3. Chop garlic, ginger and green chilli very finely and add to the saag, add shalgam if you wish. Add salt and put it on fire and let it start heating.
4. The saag will start going down. Cover and let it cook on medium fire for 15-20 minutes. Remove from fire, cool.
5. Grind to a **coarse** paste. Do not grind too much.
6. Add makki ka atta to the saag and cook for 15 minutes on low heat.
7. At serving time, heat pure ghee. Reduce heat and add ginger and green chillies. Cook till ginger changes colour. Remove from fire and add red chilli powder. Add ghee to the hot saag and mix lightly. Serve hot.
8. Serve with fresh home-made butter and makki-di-roti.

Note: Fresh saag should have tender leaves and tender stems (gandal).

Sarson Da Saag ; Makai Di Roti: Recipe on page 84 ➤

Tawa Paneer Masala

Picture on page 57 *Serves 4*

A unique preparation of cottage cheese cooked on a tawa.

MARINATE FOR 15 MINUTES
400 gms paneer (cottage cheese) - cut into big (1") cubes
½ tsp red chilli powder, ½ tsp haldi, ½ tsp salt, 1 tsp chaat masala

MASALA
½ tsp jeera (cumin seeds), ½ tsp ajwain seeds (carom seeds)
1 large onion - chopped
3 tsp garlic paste
2 green chillies - chopped
2 tsp dhania (coriander) powder
½ tsp red chilli powder
½ tsp salt, or to taste
2 tomatoes - chopped
1 capsicum - chopped
¼ tsp garam masala
¼ tsp shah jeera (black cumin)

1. Cut paneer into big, thick pieces. Sprinkle red chilli powder, haldi, salt and chaat masala. Mix well to coat all sides of paneer with the powdered masalas. Keep the marinated paneer aside for 15 minutes.
2. Heat 2 tbsp oil on a non stick tawa or a pan. Shallow fry the paneer on the tawa, turning sides, till light browned on all sides.
3. For the masala, heat 3 tbsp oil in a kadhai. When oil is hot, add ajwain and jeera. Let jeera turn golden.
3. Add the chopped onion and stir till golden.
4. Reduce heat. Add garlic paste, green chillies, coriander powder, red chilli powder, and salt. Fry on medium heat for a few seconds.
5. Add chopped tomatoes. Stir fry for 5-7 minutes till the oil separates. Keep aside.
6. Mix in the fried paneer, capsicum, garam masala & shah jeera. Mix and cook for 1-2 minutes. Serve hot.

Aloo Vadi

A thin spicy curry!

Serves 4

2 medium potatoes - cut each into 8 pieces
1 vadi (Amritsari)
½" piece ginger & 1 onion - ground to a paste
3 desi tomatoes or 3 regular tomatoes & 1 green chilli - ground to a puree
4 tbsp oil
1 tsp dhania powder
½ tsp red chilli powder
½ tsp garam masala
¼ tsp amchoor
1½ tsp salt, or to taste
¼ tsp haldi

1. Heat 4 tbsp oil in a kadhai, reduce flame. Add vadi and fry vadi, turning sides till well browned on all sides. Remove from oil and keep aside.
2. Heat the remaining oil and add the onion-ginger paste. Stir fry on medium flame till golden.
3. Remove for heat. Add haldi, dhania, red chilli powder, garam masala, amchoor and salt. Return to heat. Stir for a few seconds.
4. Add 1 tbsp water. Mix well.
5. Add the tomatoes and cook till they turn dry and oil separates.
6. Add the potatoes and 2 tbsp water. Bhuno on low heat for 3-4 minutes.
7. Add 2 cups water and the fried vadi.
8. Cook covered till potatoes are cooked.
9. Break the vadi into 4-5 pieces with a spoon and cook covered for a few more minutes till oil separates. Serve hot with rice.

Note: Curry prepared with desi tomatoes tastes better than that made with the regular tomatoes.

Khaja Aloo

Serves 8-10   *Picture on page 87*

Potatoes are simmered in a delicious, yellow gravy. Curd and cashews form the base of this curry. Black cumin lends it's royal flavour to the humble potatoes.

4 potatoes
½ tsp shah jeera (black cumin)
1 tej patta (bay leaf)
2 onions - chopped
¼ tsp haldi (turmeric)
½ tsp garam masala
2 tbsp chopped coriander
½ cup curd (yogurt) - whisked to make it smooth
oil for frying plus 4 tbsp oil

GRIND TO A PASTE
4 tbsp cashews - soaked in ¼ cup water
1 tbsp chopped ginger
1 tsp chopped garlic

1. Wash potatoes and peel. Cut potatoes into 1" pieces.
2. Fry the potatoes to a deep golden brown and keep aside.
3. Grind cashews, ginger and garlic to a paste in a small coffee or spice grinder. Keep cashew paste aside.
4. Heat 4 tbsp oil in a heavy bottomed pan. Add black cumin and bay leaf. Wait for 30 seconds till cumin stops spluttering.
5. Add onions and cook on low heat till onions turn soft but do not let them turn brown. Add haldi and garam masala. Stir to mix well.
6. Add yogurt and stir fry on low heat till water evaporates. Cook till dry.
7. Add cashew paste. Cook for 1 minute.
7. Add about 1 cup water to get a gravy. Boil and simmer for 2-3 minutes.
8. Add the fried potatoes and chopped coriander to the gravy and simmer on low heat.
9. Cook on low heat till gravy gets thick and coats the potatoes. Serve hot with rotis or paranthas.

ROTIS & CHAAWAL

Missi Roti

Makes 10

1 cup besan (gram flour)
2 cups atta (wheat flour)
1 onion - very finely chopped
2 tbsp oil or melted ghee
3/4 tsp salt, 3/4 tsp red chillies, 2 pinches of haldi
1 tsp ajwain
1 tsp anaardaana (pomegranate seeds) - whole or pounded
1 tbsp kasoori methi (dried fenugreek leaves)

1. Mix both flours. Add all other ingredients. Knead to a smooth dough of rolling consistency. Cover and keep aside for atleast 30 minutes.
2. Shape into 10 balls. Roll out each ball to a slightly thick, small chappati.
3. Cook it on hot tawa on both sides, when half done, roast on both sides on open fire. Spread white butter or pure ghee on the hot roti. Serve.

Note: Missi roti is served with fresh butter and curd and mangoes in summer. Tomato or mango chutney goes well with it.

Tandoori Roti

Makes 6-7

2 ½ cups atta (whole wheat flour)
1 cup water (approx.)
½ tsp salt
2-3 tbsp ghee

1. Keep ghee in the fridge for some time, so that it solidifies.
2. Make a soft dough with atta, salt and water. Keep aside for half an hour.
3. Divide the dough into 6 equal balls. Flatten each ball, roll out each into a round of 5" diameter.
4. Spread 1 tsp of solidified ghee. Sprinkle a teaspoon of dry flour on the ghee.
5. Make a slit, starting from any one end till almost to the other end, leaving just 1".
6. Start rolling from the slit, to form an even cone. Roll out, to a diameter of 5", applying pressure only at the centre.
7. Cook carefully in a heated tandoor till brown specs appear.

Khasta Keema Parantha

On a Sunday afternoon these paranthas served with butter milk and salad is a great favourite in many Punjabi homes.

Makes 4-5 Paranthas

1½ cups atta (wheat flour)
3/4 tsp salt
½ tsp ajwain (carom seeds)
2 tbsp ghee

STUFFING
200 gms keema (lamb mince)
3 tbsp oil/ghee
1 big onion - chopped (1 cup)
3 flakes garlic - chopped
3/4" piece ginger - chopped
4-5 green chillies - chopped (according to taste)
¼ tsp haldi, 1 tsp salt
½ tsp garam masala, ½ tsp red chilli powder
2 tbsp chopped fresh dhania

1. Mix all ingredients under dough and make a dough with water. Keep covered for ½-1 hour before making the paranthas.
2. Heat oil/ghee in a pressure cooker.
3. Add onion, garlic and ginger. Fry till onion turns brown.
4. Add green chillies, keema and all other seasonings. Fry for 4-5 minutes.
5. Add ½ cup water. Mix well. Close cooker and give 3 whistles.
6. When pressure drops, open and cook till keema is absolutely dry. Cool. Add fresh dhania and mix well.
7. Now roll out 2 small balls of the dough to 4" rounds. Spread keema filling on one roti and put the other one on top. Press the edges to seal and pat between the palms of both hands to seal the filling. Dust with dry flour and roll out carefully to a big parantha.
8. Put tawa on fire, when it is hot, place the rolled parantha on it and let it cook on both sides. Now trickle some ghee/oil from the sides to make it crisp.
9. Serve hot with butter and curds.

Note: This stuffing can be used to make keema samosas and also aloo tikkis. Boil aloo, mash and season well. Make tikkis with this stuffing. Fry and serve hot with chutney or sauce.

Makki Di Roti

Makes 6-7 *Picture on page 77*

2 cups makki ka atta (maize flour)
hot water to knead
ghee for frying

1. Sieve the flour. Knead gently with hot water to a soft dough. Do not knead the dough too much in advance.
2. Tear an old polythene bag into two halves. Keep one piece on the chakla (rolling platform). Put one ball of the kneaded dough on the polythene. Cover with the other piece of polythene, such that there is a plastic cover above and beneath the ball.
3. Roll carefully to a slightly thick roti.
4. Cook the roti on both sides on a tawa. Add some ghee and fry both sides on low flame. Serve hot with sarson da saag.

Methi Wali Makki Di Roti

Makes 6-7

2 cups makki ka atta (maize flour)
1 cup chopped fresh methi (fenugreek leaves)
1 onion - very finely chopped
2 green chillies - finely chopped
½ tsp salt, or to taste
hot water to knead the flour, ghee or oil to fry the roti

1. Sieve the flour. Wash, remove the stems and chop the methi leaves.
2. Mix the chopped methi in the flour, add salt, chopped onions and green chillies
3. Just before making the rotis, knead the flour with hot water to a smooth dough. Do not knead the dough too much in advance.
4. Tear an old polythene bag into two halves. Keep one piece on the chakla (rolling platform).
5. Put one ball of the kneaded dough on the polythene. Cover with the other piece, such that there is a plastic cover above and beneath the ball. Roll carefully to a slightly thick roti.
6. Heat the tawa (griddle). Put the roti on the hot tawa and cook on both sides, and fry the roti like parantha on low flame.

Matar Vadi Wale Chaawal

Serves 4

1-2 vadis (of moong or urad dal)
1 cup shelled peas
1 cup basmati rice - soaked for 1 hour
4 tbsp oil
1 tsp jeera (cumin seeds), 2 moti illaichi (brown cardamoms)
4 laung (cloves), 1 tej patta (bay leaf)
1" piece ginger - cut into matchsticks
1¼ tsp salt, or to taste, juice of ½ lemon

1. Drain soaked rice and keep ready.
2. Heat oil in a heavy bottomed pan. Reduce flame. Add vadi and fry turning sides till well browned all over. Remove from oil and keep aside.
3. Heat remaining oil. Add jeera, moti illaichi, laung and tej patta.
4. When jeera turns golden, add ginger and peas. Fry for 1 minute.
5. Break vadi into small pieces.
6. Add rice & the broken vadis. Fry for 2 minutes on low heat, stirring gently.
7. Add 2 cups water, salt and lemon juice. Boil. After one boil cover tightly and lower heat. Cook for about 8-10 minutes, till all the water is used and the rice well cooked.

Bhature

Makes 8   *Picture on page 2*

2 cups maida (plain flour)
1 cup suji (semolina)
½ tsp soda-bicarb, ½ tsp salt
½ tsp sugar, ½ cup sour curd
oil for deep frying

1. Soak suji in water, which is just enough to cover it. Keep aside for 10 minutes.
2. Sift salt, soda and maida in a paraat. Add sugar, soaked suji and curd.
3. Knead with enough warm water to make a dough of rolling consistency.
4. Knead again with greased hands till the dough is smooth.
5. Brush the dough with oil. Keep the dough in a greased polythene and keep it in a warm place for 3-4 hours.
6. Make 8-10 balls. Roll each ball to an oblong shape. Deep fry in hot oil. Serve.

Keemae De Chaawal

Rice with minced mutton.

Serves 5-6

1½ cups basmati rice
400 gms keema (lamb mince)
2 large or 4 small potatoes - peeled and cut into small ¼" cubes (2 cups)
6-7 tbsp ghee
2-3 laung (cloves)
5-6 saboot kali mirch (black peppercorns)
1" piece dalchini (cinnamon)
1 tej patta (bay leaf)
2 big onions - sliced (2 cups)
2½ tsp ginger paste
3½ tsp salt
2½ tsp red chilli powder (Kashmiri) - adjust to taste
3/4 tsp haldi powder
1 tsp garam masala powder
4 tbsp fresh dhania - chopped
10-12 poodina (mint) leaves

1. In a pressure cooker heat ghee.
2. Add laung, kali mirch, dalchini and tej patta. Fry for 1 minute.
3. Add sliced onions and fry till light brown.
4. Add ginger paste. Fry for 1 minute.
5. Add keema and potato cubes and all the seasonings. Fry well till ghee comes out.
6. Add washed rice, dhania and mint. Fry for 1-2 minutes.
7. Add 3 cups water. Mix well.
8. Close cooker and give 2 whistles. Remove from fire.
9. When the pressure drops, open the cooker and fluff rice with a fork. Serve hot garnished with tomato and lemon wedges with curd and achaar.

Khaja Aloo : Recipe on page 80 ➤

Chicken Kali Mirch Pulao

A delicious pulao with the colour and fragrance of pepper. Freshly ground pepper gives a better flavour. Served with kachumber (minced salad) and yogurt, it makes a complete meal.

Serves 8

3 cups basmati rice
1 chicken (1 kg) - cut into pieces of your choice
2 cups peas
8 tbsp oil
5 tbsp pure ghee
1½ tsp jeera (cumin seeds)
12 saboot kali mirch (peppercorns)
3 moti illaichi (black cardamoms)
2" piece dalchini (cinnamon)
2 tej patta (bay leaves)
4 large onions - sliced
2 tsp ginger paste
2 tsp garlic paste
3½ tsp salt
3 tsp black pepper powder - freshly powdered
2 tsp garam masala powder
4 tbsp finely chopped fresh dhania
4 tbsp lemon juice

1. Heat ghee and oil. Add jeera, kali mirch, moti illaichi, tej patta and dalchini. Fry till jeera turns brown.
2. Add sliced onions and fry till onion becomes dark brown.
3. Add ginger and garlic paste. Fry for 1-2 minutes.
4. Add chicken, peas, salt, pepper, garam masala and fresh dhania. Fry for 8-10 minutes. Cover on low heat for 5-6 minutes.
5. Add lemon juice and 6 cups of water.
6. When water boils add washed rice.
7. Mix well. Cover and lower heat. Cook for approximately 20 minutes or till rice is cooked and all the water has been absorbed.
8. Fluff rice with a fork and serve hot garnished with finely chopped tomatoes and fresh coriander.

Gobi De Paranthe

Makes 8

2½ cups atta (wheat flour)
1 large cauliflower - washed and grated
3 green chillies - deseeded and chopped finely
2 tbsp coriander leaves - chopped
1" piece ginger - grated
½ tsp ajwain (carom seeds)
1½ tsp salt, or to taste
½ tsp red chilli powder
½ tsp garam masala
1 tsp anardaana (pomegranate seeds) - pounded
cooking oil or ghee for frying

1. Knead the flour to a smooth dough and keep it aside for atleast 15 minutes.
2. Remove stem and break cauliflower into florets, wash the cauliflower. Wipe with a clean kitchen towel. Grate finely. Add all the ingredients - chopped chillies, coriander, ginger and dry masalas.
3. Roll out 2 small balls of flour into 4" diameter, spread cauliflower filling generously on one roti and put the other one on top. Press the edges to seal and pat between the palms of both the hands to seal the filling. Roll in dry flour and roll out carefully to a big parantha.
4. Put tawa on fire, when it gets hot, put rolled out parantha on it and let it cook on both sides and then trickle some ghee or oil from the sides to get crisp edges. Serve with fresh white butter and curds.

Mooli De Paranthe

Wash, peel and grate radish. Sprinkle some salt and keep aside for 15 minutes to sweat. Squeeze out water and add the other ingredients. Do not discard the mooli water, use it for making the dough for the paranthas. You get tangier paranthas if the mooli water is used for making the dough. Make paranthas the same way as gobi de paranthe. You may also finely chop 1-2 leaves of the mooli and add to the grated radish if you like.

Champae Waale Chaawal

Serves 4-5

300 gms mutton ribs (champae) - 4 pieces
1½ cups rice - washed and strained and kept in the strainer for 15 minutes after washing, do not soak rice
3 tbsp ghee
3 tbsp oil
2-3 saboot kali mirch (black peppercorns)
1 moti illaichi (black cardamom)
2-3 laung (cloves)
1" dalchini (cinnamon)
1 tej patta (bay leaf)
2 medium onions - sliced
3 flakes garlic - chopped
3/4" piece ginger - chopped
2 tomatoes - chopped
2½ tsp salt
1 tsp garam masala
1¼ tsp Kashmiri red chilli powder

GARNISH
1 egg - hard boiled and cut into wedges
some fresh coriander

1. Heat oil and ghee in a pressure cooker. Add saboot kali mirch, moti illaichi, laung, dalchini and tej patta. Fry for 1 minute.
2. Add sliced onions, garlic and ginger and fry till onions turn soft.
3. Add mutton, tomatoes, salt, garam masala powder and red chill powder. Fry for 8-10 minutes.
4. Add 1½ cups water and pressure cook to give 1 whistle. Keep on low heat for 20 minutes. Remove from fire. After the pressure drops, dry the water on fire.
5. Add washed rice. Fry for 1 minute. Add 3 cups water. Mix well.
6. Close the cooker and give 3 whistles.
7. When the pressure drops, check if rice is dry, (water is absorbed by the rice).
8. Fluff rice with a fork and serve hot garnished with fresh coriander and hard boiled egg wedges.

Poodina Parantha

Makes 8

2 cups atta (whole wheat flour)
2 tbsp poodina (mint leaves), freshly chopped or dry
1 tsp ajwain (carom seeds)
2 tbsp ghee
½ tsp salt, ½ tsp red chilli powder

1. Mix atta with all ingredients except poodina. Add enough water to make a dough of rolling consistency. Cover and keep the dough aside for 30 minutes.
2. Make walnut sized balls. Roll out a little to make a thick chappati.
3. Spread 1 tsp ghee all over. Fold a little from the left and then right to meet in the centre. Fold the top and the bottom to now get a square.
4. Roll out to get a square parantha, but do not make it too thin. Sprinkle poodina. Press with the belan (rolling pin).
5. Cook on a tawa, frying on both sides till crisp and well browned.

Quick Peethi Poori

Makes 12

1 cup atta (whole wheat flour)
1 tsp oil or melted ghee, ½ tsp salt
¼ cup urad dal - soaked for 2 hours and coarsely ground to get peethi
or ½ cup ready made dal ki peethi, 1 tsp suji (semolina)
½ tsp salt, 1 tsp kuti laal mirch (red chilli flakes), ¼ tsp ajwain (carom seeds)

1. Sift flour and ½ tsp salt together and rub in melted ghee or oil.
2. Knead to a little stiff dough with about 3/4-1 cup water and set aside.
3. Mix dal ki peethi with ½ tsp salt, 1 tsp kuti laal mirch, ¼ tsp ajwain, 1 tsp suji.
4. Divide dough into small balls and roll out the balls into small poories.
5. Spread 1 tsp full peethi on the rolled out poori with the spoon. The peethi is spread on the outside of the puri instead of stuffing it within.
6. Heat oil, drop the rolled poories gently into it **with the peethi side down in the oil,** so that the dal gets cooked in the hot oil.
7. Press the sides of the poori with a perforated frying spoon and make the poori swell up. Turn. Fry till golden brown and crisp. Drain on brown paper.

Note: The peethi can be stuffed inside the poori also.

Amritsari Nan

Picture on back cover   Makes 6

2½ cups (250 gms) maida (plain flour), ½ tsp salt
½ cup hot milk, 1 tsp baking powder
½ cup warm water (approx)
10 badaam (almonds) - skinned & cut into long thin pieces (slivered (cut into thin long pieces))
1 tbsp kasoori methi

1. Heat milk and put it in a paraat or a large pan. Add baking powder to the hot milk. Mix well and keep it aside for 1-2 minutes till it starts to bubble.
2. Sift maida and salt together. Add maida to the hot milk. Mix.
3. Knead to a dough with enough warm water.
4. Keep in a warm place for 3-4 hours.
5. Make 6-8 balls. Roll out each ball to an oblong shape. Spread ghee all over. Fold one side (lengthways) a little, so as to overlap an inch of the nan. Press lightly on the joint with the belan (rolling pin).
6. Sprinkle some kasoori methi and blanched (skin removed by dipping in hot water) and chopped almonds. Press with a rolling pin (belan). Pull one side of the nan to give it a pointed end like the shape of the nan.
7. Apply some water on the back side of the nan. Stick in a hot gas tandoor.
8. Cook till nan is ready. Spread butter on the ready nan and serve hot.

Keema Nan

FILLING
250 gm keema (minced meat)
3 tbsp oil, 1 onion - chopped finely, 2 tsp ginger - chopped finely
1 tsp salt, 1 tsp dhania powder, ½ tsp red chilli powder, ½ tsp garam masala
2 green chillies - chopped, 1 tbsp finely chopped fresh coriander
1 tsp kale til (black sesame seeds) - to sprinkle on top

1. Make the dough as for Amritsari nan and keep aside for 3-4 hours.
2. To prepare the filling, heat 3 tbsp of oil and fry the chopped onion until rich brown. Add keema (mince) and ginger and mix well. Reduce heat. Add salt, dhania powder, red chilli powder and garam masala. Fry for 1-2 minutes. Cook covered on low heat for about 5 minutes, till the mince is cooked.
3. Add green chillies and 1 tbsp finely chopped coriander. If there is any water, uncover and dry the mince on fire. Keep the stuffing aside.

4. Make 6-8 balls from the dough. Make a cup of each ball and fill 1 tbsp filling. Roll out to an oblong shape.
5. Sprinkle some black sesame seeds and press them with a belan.
6. Pull one side of the nan to give it a pointed end like the shape of the nan.
7. Apply some water on the back side of the nan. Stick in a hot gas tandoor.
8. Cook till nan is ready. Spread some butter on the ready nan and serve hot.

Lachha Parantha

Makes 6 *Picture on cover*

3 cups atta (whole wheat flour)
3-4 tbsp ghee
½ tsp salt

1. Mix atta with ghee and salt. Sprinkle water and knead well to a non sticky dough. Set aside for 1 hour.
2. Knead again and make 6 big balls, the size of an onion. Roll out each to a diameter of 8", almost as big as the chakla.
3. Spread 1 tsp full softened ghee all over. Sprinkle some dry atta on the ghee.
4. Pleat the chappati lengthwise into one collected strip.
5. Twist this strip.
6. Coil the strip to get a pedha (round flattened ball).

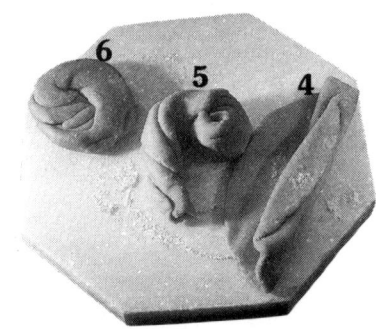

7. Flatten this ball between the palms of the hands or gently roll on the chakla (rolling board) with the belan (rolling pin) without applying too much pressure, to a small thick parantha of about 6" diameter.
8. Cook in a tandoor by applying water on the back side of the parantha. If you like you can cook it on a hot tawa also. To cook on a tawa first make both the sides light brown on a hot tawa. Reduce flame and then using ghee fry till rich brown on both sides on low heat. Press the sides and all over the parantha with a spoon while frying to ensure that it gets cooked since the parantha is a little thick.
9. Remove from tawa on to a clean kitchen napkin and press the hot parantha on the cloth from all sides for the layers to open up and turn flaky. Serve hot.

SNACKS

Reshmi Kababs

Delicious chicken kababs that are excellent for cocktails and dinners. Remember to marinate the kebabs for atleast 5-6 hours in the refrigerator to get really soft kebabs.

Serves 7-8

600 gms boneless chicken or 600 gms of chicken breasts - cut into 2" pieces
2 tbsp butter plus 2 tbsp oil
4 tbsp besan (gram flour)
2 tsp ginger paste
2 tsp garlic paste
2 tsp green chilli paste (adjust to taste)
2 tbsp green fresh coriander paste
1½ tsp salt
¼ cup curd (thick)
½ cup fresh cream
1 egg
4 tbsp lemon juice

1. Heat oil and butter in a kadhai/non stick pan. Add besan and cook till a nice smell comes and besan turns medium brown.
2. Add ginger, garlic and green chilli paste. Cook stirring all the time for 1-2 minutes. Remove from heat and let it cool.
3. Add salt, curd, cream, egg, lemon juice and coriander leaf paste to the roasted besan and mix well.
4. Marinate chicken in this for 5-6 hours. Cover with a cling film and keep in a refrigerator.
5. Heat oven to 180°C. Brush the wire rack or grill of the oven with oil. Place chicken pieces on it and grill them for about 15 minutes. Baste the kababs with melted butter/oil once in between after about 8 minutes and overturn them also. Grill till the coating turns dry.
6. Serve hot with lemon wedges, onion rings and mint chutney.

Note:

1. The kababs should not brown too much. Adjust the grill so that the flame is not too close to the kababs.
2. A little dalchini powder can be added to the marinade for a different flavour.
3. Number of people served by this recipe depends on the appetite of your guests.

Paneer Pakore (Special)

Serves 4

250 gm paneer
some chaat masala to sprinkle

FILLING
½ tsp ajwain
1 small onion - grated and squeezed
1" ginger piece - grated and crushed to a paste
3-4 flakes garlic - crushed
½ tsp chilli powder, ½ tsp garam masala, ½ tsp salt
1 tsp dhania powder, 1 tsp amchoor

BATTER
1 cup besan
1/3 cup water - approx.
2 pinches baking powder
3/4 tsp each red chilli powder and salt, or to taste
2 tbsp chopped coriander

1. Cut paneer into 1½" squares which are slightly thicker than ¼" thickness.
2. Slit the pieces of paneer, a little more than halfway but not till the end.
3. Sprinkle some chaat masala on them on both sides.
4. To prepare the filling, mix grated and squeezed onion and ginger, garlic pastes. Add all other masalas.
5. With the help of the knife insert some filling in the paneer pieces. Press well.
6. Prepare a thick batter with all the given ingredients. Beat well and keep aside for 10 minutes.
7. Dip the stuffed pieces of paneer in the batter and deep fry in hot oil till golden.
8. Serve hot sprinkled with chaat masala.

Matar Khumba Curry: Recipe on page 75 ➤

Chicken Tikka

Serves 4

2-3 breasts of chicken or 500 gm boneless chicken - cut into 2" pieces (8-12 pieces)
some chaat masala, lemon juice and coriander leaves

1ST MARINADE
2 tbsp vinegar or lemon juice
¼ tsp salt
½ tsp chilli powder

2ND MARINADE
6 tbsp thick hung curd (hang about 3/4 cup curd)
2-3 tbsp thick malai or cream
2 tsp ginger-garlic paste
¼ tsp black salt, ½ tsp garam masala powder
¼ tsp red chilli powder, 3/4-1 tsp salt, or to taste
2-3 drops of red colour
melted butter to baste

1. Wash the chicken pieces and pat dry on a kitchen towel.
2. Marinate the pieces in the 1st marinade for ½ hour.
3. In a bowl mix curd, cream, ginger-garlic paste, black salt, garam masala, red chill powder, colour and salt.
4. Remove the chicken pieces from the 1st marinade. Pat dry slightly. Add to the curd mixture and marinate for 6-8 hours in the refrigerator.
5. Heat a gas tandoor on gas or an electric oven at 180°C. Place the well coated chicken pieces on the grill or skewer the chicken pieces. Grill for about 10 minutes or until cooked, thoroughly basting with melted butter or oil atleast once in between.
6. Sprinkle with chaat masala and lemon juice.
7. Serve hot garnished with onion rings and coriander leaves.

Besan Di Murgi

Serves 3-4

400 gms chicken - cut into pieces or 6 legs (drumsticks)
3/4 cup milk
1 tsp red chilli powder, 3/4 tsp salt

GRIND TOGETHER TO A PASTE
½" piece ginger
2-3 flakes garlic
2 saboot kali mirch (peppercorns)
2 laung (cloves)
2 chhoti illaichi (green cardamoms)
1 tsp jeera (cumin seeds)
2 tsp saboot dhania (coriander seeds)
3/4" stick dalchini
3/4 tsp saunf (fennel)

COATING
8 tbsp besan
6 tbsp curd
1 tbsp chopped fresh dhania
½ tsp salt, ¼ tsp red chilli powder
¼ tsp ajwain (carom seeds)

1. Grind together ginger, garlic along with all the saboot masalas. Use a little water if required. Keep the ground masala aside.
2. Mix together 3/4 cup milk with ¼ cup water. Heat and bring to a boil.
3. Add the above ground masala, 1 tsp red chilli powder and 3/4 tsp salt.
4. Add chicken also to the milk. Give 1-2 boils. Cover and lower heat. Cook for 8-10 minutes or till chicken is tender. Increase heat and cook till completely dry. Remove from fire. Cool.
5. To the cooked chicken add all the coating ingredients. Mix well.
6. Heat oil and fry 2-3 pieces at a time to a golden brown colour.
7. Serve hot with mint chutney, onion rings and lemon wedges

Note: Chops/Ribs can also be cooked in this manner. Only at stage 4, after 1-2 boils, give 2-3 whistles in a pressure cooker to ensure that the ribs get tender.

Punjabi Aloo Tikki

Makes 10

½ kg (6 medium) potatoes - boiled and mashed
2 tbsp cornflour
1 tsp salt
ghee or oil for shallow frying

FILLING
1/3 cup channa dal (Bengal gram)
½ tsp jeera (cumin seeds)
½" piece ginger - finely chopped
salt to taste
2 green chillies - finely chopped
½ tsp red chillies
½ tsp chaat masala
½ tsp garam masala
1 tbsp coriander leaves - chopped

1. Soak channe ki dal for 3-4 hours.
2. Heat 1 tbsp oil or ghee in a kadhai. Add jeera, allow to splutter. Add chopped green chillies, red chillies and salt.
3. Drain dal and add to the kadhai. Cover and let it cook on low heat till it turns soft and gets cooked. Sprinkle some water while it is being cooked.
4. Cook dal till soft and dry. Add chaat masala, garam masala and chopped coriander leaves. Remove from fire and keep aside to cool.
5. Boil, peel and mash potatoes. Add 2 tbsp cornflour and 1 tsp salt.
6. Grease the palm of your right hand. Take a ball of mashed potatoes on the oiled palm. Make a shallow cup with the ball of mashed potatoes.
7. Place a tbsp of dal filling in the centre and seal well to form a ball. Flatten the ball to form a tikki.
7. Heat oil on a tawa or a frying pan. Shallow fry 2-3 tikkis at a time till well browned and crisp on both sides.
8. Serve hot with imli and poodina chutney.

Murg Haryali Kababs

Delicious fried chicken, flavoured with green chutney. These can be grilled too.

Serves 6

1 chicken (1 kg) - cut into 2" pieces or only chicken legs or breasts can be used
4 tbsp besan (gram flour), 1½ tsp salt
oil for frying

GRIND TO A FINE PASTE
1 cup fresh dhania, 2 tsp saunf (fennel)
5-6 flakes garlic, 1" piece ginger, 6 tbsp lemon juice

1. Grind together dhania, saunf, ginger, garlic and lemon juice to a fine paste.
2. Mix together ground paste, besan and salt.
3. Prick chicken all over with a fork or give shallow cuts with a knife.
4. Rub the marinade all over the chicken pieces. Leave to marinate for 2-3 hours or in the fridge for 6-8 hours or overnight.
5. Heat oil and fry chicken pieces to a rich colour. Check chicken for tenderness and crispness before removing from oil. Drain on a paper napkin.
6. Serve hot garnished with onion and tomato rings.

Note: For a different flavour, grind ½ cup poodina (mint) leaves along with the other ingredients.

Haryali Paneer Tikka

Serves 6   *Picture on page 1*

400 gm paneer - cut into 1½" pieces, 1" thick
4 tbsp besan (gram flour), 1 tsp salt, 4 tbsp oil

GRIND TO A FINE PASTE (CHUTNEY)
1 cup fresh green dhania, 2 tsp saunf (fennel)
5-6 flakes garlic, 1" piece ginger, 6 tbsp lemon juice, ½ tsp salt

1. Grind together dhania, saunf, ginger, garlic, lemon juice and salt to a fine paste.
2. Slit the paneer piece. Divide the chutney into 2 equal portions. Use one part to stuff some chutney in the slits of all the paneer pieces.
3. Mix together the left over chutney, besan, salt and oil. Rub this all over the stuffed paneer pieces. Place paneer on a greased wire rack of the oven.
4. Grill in a hot oven at 180°C for 15 minutes. Spoon some drops of oil on the paneer pieces and grill further for 5 minutes. Serve hot.

Dahi Bhalle

Makes 15

1½ cups (250 gm) urad dal - washed and soaked in enough water for 3 hours
½" piece ginger - very finely chopped
2 green chillies - chopped
½ tsp salt
¼ tsp soda-bicarb
½ tsp jeera (cumin seeds)
some chopped coriander - to garnish
oil for frying

DAHI (CURD)
3 cups curds - beat well till smooth
½ tsp powdered sugar
½ tsp red chilli powder, salt to taste
1 tsp bhuna jeera powder
¼ tsp kala namak

1. Wash and soak dal in enough water to cover the dal.
2. Soak it for 3 hours. Drain water and grind with the minimum amount of water to a paste. Do not over grind and make it too smooth.
3. Add finely chopped ginger, green chillies and salt.
4. Add soda and beat well for 4-5 minutes till the mixture turns whitish and frothy. It is better to use an electric hand mixer for beating. Add 2-3 tbsp hot water while beating.
5. Heat oil. With moistened hands, make bhalla with dal batter into 2" discs. Sprinkle some jeera seeds on it. Press lightly to stick the jeera and flatten the bhalla.
6. Deep fry 5-6 bhallas at a time in hot oil till they swell. Reduce heat to medium and turn the side. Fry on low medium heat till light golden. Drain from oil, keep aside.
7. Boil 6 cups water with 2 tsp salt. Remove water from fire and add the bhallas. Soak bhallas in salted hot water for 5 minutes.
8. Press out water lightly and arrange bhallas in a flat dish.
9. Beat curd. Add all the ingredients to the curd. Pour curds on the arranged bhallas. Garnish with red chilli powder, chopped coriander and bhuna jeera powder. Serve with imli chutney and extra beaten curd.

Chicken Lollipops

A delicious snack made from chicken wings. The lollipops look like mini dumb bells. Remember to cover the end of the bone of the lollipops with a piece of foil.

Serves 3-4

600 gms lollipops

MIX TOGETHER
1½ tsp ginger paste
1½ tsp garlic paste
1 tsp salt
1½ tsp Kashmiri red chilli powder (degi mirch)
2 tsp amchoor powder
1 tsp garam masala
a pinch of tandoori red colour
4 tbsp maida
oil for frying

1. Mix all the ingredients together.
2. Mix the lollipops in the mixture and let them marinate for 3-4 hours in the refrigerator.
3. At the time of serving, shape each piece to give them a neat look.
4. Shallow fry in a pan in 5-6 tbsp oil, turning sides or deep fry a few at a time till tender & crisp. If you shallow fry, keep the pan covered so that the chicken gets done while frying.
4. Drain on a paper napkin.
5. Serve on a bed of onion rings along with lemon wedges.

Shami Kababs

A great favourite of Punjabis. Whenever you are invited to a Punjabi home for tea or cocktails, these kababs will always be made.

Gives 30-32 Kababs

500 gms keema/mutton mince
8 tbsp channa dal
8 tbsp oil
2 onions - chopped finely
7-8 flakes garlic - chopped
1½" piece ginger - chopped fine
3-4 green chillies - chopped (optional)
1" dalchini (cinnamon)
6-7 laung (cloves)
1 tej patta (bay leaf)
6-7 chhoti illaichi (green cardamoms)
2 moti illaichi (black cardamoms)
2 tsp salt
2 tsp red chilli powder (Kashmiri)
1 tsp garam masala
1 egg
oil for frying

1. Heat oil in a cooker. Add dalchini, laung, tej patta and both illaichis. Fry for 1 minute.
2. Add onion, ginger, garlic and green chillies. Fry till onion turns light brown.
3. Add keema, salt, chillies, garam masala and washed channa dal. Fry for 5 minutes.
4. Add 1 cup water, close the cooker and give 3 whistles. Remove from fire.
5. When pressure drops, open and cook till keema is absolutely dry. Cool.
6. Remove all the khada (saboot) garam masalas.
7. Grind keema in a mixer to a fine paste.
8. Add egg and mix well. Keep in the fridge for 1-2 hours.
9. Shape into small kababs and deep fry to a deep brown colour.
10. Serve hot with mint chutney on a bed of onion rings mixed with fresh lemon juice and chopped fresh dhania.

Gobi Pakore (Special)

Serves 6

1 gobi (cauliflower) - cut into medium florets with stalks
1 tsp each salt & red chilli, 1 tsp ajwain, 1 tbsp ginger paste, 1 tsp garlic paste

BATTER
1½ cups besan (gram flour), 2 pinches baking powder, 1 tsp salt
1 tsp red chilli powder, a pinch of haldi, ½ cup water - approx.

1. Boil 3-4 cups water with 1 tsp salt. Add cauliflower and remove from fire. Let the cauliflower be in hot water for 10 minutes. Strain. Sprinkle salt & red chilli powder on the cauliflower. Keep aside for 15 minutes and drain out the water. Pat dry on a clean kitchen towel.
2. Rub ginger, garlic paste & ajwain on the cauliflower and keep aside.
3. Prepare a thick pouring batter with all the ingredients using enough water. Beat well to a smooth consistency. Keep aside for 10 minutes.
4. Heat oil. Dip the cauliflower pieces in the batter and deep fry to a light golden colour on low medium flame. Remove from oil and keep aside.
5. At serving time, press the pakoras to flatten slightly and refry in medium hot oil till well browned and crisp.

Amritsari Paneer

Serves 4

250 gms paneer - cut into thin fingers
2 tbsp ginger-garlic paste
½ tsp ajwain
a few drops of orange colour
½ tsp each salt and red chilli powder
4-5 tbsp besan
oil for frying
chaat masala to sprinkle

1. Mix ginger-garlic paste with ajwain, colour, salt and red chilli powder.
2. Marinate the paneer fingers with this paste. Keep aside till serving time.
3. At serving time, heat oil for frying. Sprinkle besan on the paneer fingers and mix lightly to coat the paneer with besan.
5. Deep fry till crisp. Serve sprinkled generously with chaat masala.

Tandoori Chicken

An all time favourite of not only Punjabis but all people fond of good food.

Picture on facing page   Serves 4-5

1 chicken (1 kg) - cut into 8 pieces
6 tbsp curd
2 tbsp maida (plain flour)
a pinch of orange red colour
1 tsp garlic paste, 1 tsp ginger paste
1½ tsp salt, ½ tsp jeera powder
½ tsp dhania powder, 1 tsp red chilli powder
½ tsp garam masala powder, 1½ tsp amchoor powder

1. Mix curd, maida, colour and all other ingredients. Add enough colour to get a bright orange colour.
2. Wash chicken. Squeeze out all excess water. Pat dry on a clean kitchen towel.
3. Marinate chicken in the curd mixture for 2-3 hours in the refrigerator.
4. Rub the wire rack of the oven with oil and place the marinated chicken on it, so that the extra marinade can drip down from the grill. If the chicken is placed in a dish or a tray, the extra marinade and liquid keep collecting around the chicken pieces and hence they do not turn dry and crisp.
5. Grill for 8-10 minutes in an oven at 180°C.
6. Overturn again, brush with oil and grill for another 10-12 minutes or till tender and crisp. Serve hot garnished with onion rings and lemon wedges.

Note:

1. Instead of a full chicken only drumsticks (legs) can be made. They are called tangdi kababs. After grilling, wrap a piece of aluminium foil at the end of each leg. Besides looking nice, it is also convenient for holding and eating the chicken leg.
2. Boneless chicken cut into 1½"-2" pieces can be cooked in a similar manner to get chicken tikka.
3. The grilled chicken can be added to an onion-tomato masala for a tikka masala dish.
4. For chicken tikka, in the marinade instead of maida, besan can be added for a different flavour.
5. Fish tikka is also made this way. Use boneless and skinless 2" - 3" pieces of fish.

Fish Tikka

Serves 6-8

500 gm boneless Singhara or Sole fish - cut into 2" cubes

1ST MARINADE
2 tbsp vinegar or lemon juice
¼ tsp red chilli powder
½ tsp salt

2ND MARINADE
2 tbsp hung curd (hang 4 heaped tbsp curd to get 2 tbsp)
2 tbsp thick cream or malai
1 tsp ginger-garlic paste
½ tsp garam masala powder
½ tsp ajwain (carom seeds)
½ tsp salt & ¼ tsp chilli powder, or to taste

FOR GARNISHING
lemon slices, mint or coriander sprig, some chat masala

1. Wash and pat dry the tikka pieces on a kitchen towel.
2. Marinate with lemon juice, salt and red chilli powder. Keep aside for ½ hour.
3. In a bowl mix curd, cream, ginger-garlic paste, garam masala, ajwain, salt & red chilli powder.
4. Add tikka pieces and coat well with this marinade. Keep aside for 3-4 hours.
5. Heat a gas tandoor on gas or an electric oven to 180°C.
6. Skewer tikkas or place them on the grill (brush grill with oil) and grill till coating turns dry and golden brown. Baste with a little melted butter in between.
7. Serve hot garnished with lemon wedges and coriander. Sprinkle some chaat masala.

Malai Kababs

Delicious kababs that will melt in your mouth with the distinct flavour of cardamoms.

No. of people served by this recipe depends on the appetite of your guests. Men/Boys will consume much more particularly if they are served with drinks at a cocktail.

Serves 6-7

500 gms boneless chicken - cut into 1½" pieces or 500 gms of chicken breasts (3) - cut into 2" pieces

MARINADE
¼ cup fresh cream
1 tsp garlic paste
2 tsp ginger paste
½ tsp garam masala powder
¼ tsp amchoor
½ tsp jeera powder
1½ tsp salt
¼ tsp green cardamom powder (seeds of 2-3 cardamoms crushed)
2 green chillies - ground, optional
1½ tsp white pepper powder - adjust to taste

1. Mix together cream, ginger & garlic paste and all other ingredients to form the marinade.
2. Marinate chicken for 5-6 hours in the refrigerator, covered with a cling film.
3. Heat oven to 180°C. Brush the wire rack or grill of the oven with oil. Place chicken pieces on it and grill them for 15-18 minutes overturning them every few minutes till they are nice and tender. Grill till the coating turns dry. Baste the kababs with melted butter/oil every few minutes.

Note:

1. For a different flavour 1 tsp saunf (fennel) powder can be added to the marinade.
2. There is no need for basting as cream is present in the marinade but basting every few minutes with oil or melted butter produces a glossier and softer kababs.

AACHAAR

Sirke Waale Pyaaz

Serves 4-6

12-13 small onions
½ cup white vinegar, ½ cup water
1 tsp salt, ½ tsp red chilli powder

1. Peel onions. Make a cross slit on each onion on the top.
2. Place in a bowl. Sprinkle salt and chilli powder on them and rub well.
3. Boil water and vinegar together in a pan. Remove from fire.
4. Pour the hot vinegar water over the onions in the bowl.
5. When the vinegar cools a little, transfer the onions and vinegar into a clean bottle. Keep in the refrigerator.
6. Use after a day.

Note: A few ginger match sticks and green chillies can also be added.

Khatti Arbi da Salaad

Serves 2-3

250 gm arbi (colocasia)
½ tsp salt, or to taste
¼ tsp red chilli powder, ½ tsp chaat masala
1 green chilli - deseeded and chopped
2-3 tbsp chopped coriander
juice of 1 lemon

1. Boil and peel arbi. Cut into round slices of ¼" thickness.
2. Add salt, chilli powder and chaat masala. Mix.
3. Add green chillies and coriander.
4. Sprinkle juice of ½ lemon. Toss well to mix. Use forks for mixing. Cover and keep aside till serving time.
5. At serving time sprinkle some more lemon juice and mix lightly. Serve at room temperature.

Khatta Mitha Kukkad Achaar

A delicious sweet & sour pickle. Eat with roti, rice or bread. It comes in very handy when unexpected guests drop in.

Serves 5-6

1 chicken (1 kg) - cut into pieces of your choice
10-12 tbsp mustard oil
2 large onions
10-12 large flakes garlic
1½ tsp red chilli powder (Kashmiri - as it gives better colour)
1½ tsp salt
100 gms gur (jaggery)
1 cup vinegar

DRY ROAST AND GRIND ROUGHLY
2 tsp saunf (fennel)
1 tsp methi dal

1. Grind together onion and garlic to a fine paste.
2. On a tawa dry roast saunf and methi dal. Grind to a coarse powder.
3. Heat mustard oil till it smokes. Remove from fire. Cool.
4. Now heat oil a little again. Add onion paste. Fry to a rich brown colour.
5. Add chicken and fry till it changes colour.
6. To the chicken add, salt and red chilli powder. Fry for 3-4 minutes. Cover. Lower heat and let it cook for 10-12 minutes. Remove from fire when the chicken turns tender. Keep aside.
7. In another vessel mix gur and vinegar. Heat and keep stirring till the gur dissolves completely. Keep aside.
8. When chicken is tender add vinegar and gur mixture to it. Mix well. Give 1-2 boils and remove from heat.
9. Cool. Add saunf and methi dal powder. Mix well.
9. Cool completely and store in an air tight container. Serve as and when required.

Note:

1. As this is an achaar, care should be taken that no water is used in its preparation and no water touches it after it is prepared or it will get spoilt.
2. After 1-2 days I prefer to keep it in the fridge, where it stays for quite some time.

Gobi Shalgam Da Achaar

2½ kg - gobi, carrots and shalgam (all 3 vegetables mixed together)
100 gm garlic - ground to a paste
100 gm ginger - ground to paste
100 gm rai powder
3-4 tsp haldi
100 gms red chillies (for a hot pickle, add more chillies)
500 gm gur (jaggery)
2 cups (500 ml) vinegar
500 gm mustard oil
25 gm kasoori methi (dried fenugreek leaves)

1. Peel carrots and shalgam (turnips). Cut carrots into fingers, shalgam into round slices and gobi (cauliflower) into medium sized florets.
2. Boil water in a big pan. Add vegetables. Remove from fire immediately. Let the vegetables be in the hot water for ½ hour. Keep aside.
3. After ½ hour remove the vegetables from the water with a slotted spoon and dry them on a clean cloth in the shade.
4. Next day, heat oil to smoking point, reduce flame. Add garlic paste and fry till light golden in colour.
5. Add ginger paste & fry till light brown. Remove from fire.
6. Add salt, rai powder, kasoori methi, red chilli powder and haldi to the ginger-garlic mixture.
7. Smear the dried vegetables kept in a large pan, with this masala & transfer them in a jar.
8. In a clean dry pan heat vinegar, add gur to it and cook till gur dissolves. Strain it, cool and add it to the pickle in the jar. Shake well so that it mixes evenly with the vegetables.
9. Keep the pickle in the sun for 4-5 days.

Note:

1. If you want the pickle to be sweet, reduce the chillies and increase the gur according to taste.
2. If you like the pickle to be soft, boil the vegetables for 2-3 minutes and then remove from fire.

Kachalu Da Achaar

1 kg kachalu (yam)
100 gm saunf (fennel seeds)
100 gm salt
100 gm rai powder
100 gm methi daana (fenugreek seeds)
2 tsp haldi
4 to 6 tsp red chilli powder
250 gm mustard oil
1 cup vinegar

1. Boil the whole kachaalu for 10 minutes till it feels soft when a knife is inserted into it.
2. Peel and cut into medium sized pieces. Dry on a muslin cloth in the shade.
3. Heat oil. Cool it. Add all the masalas and mix kachaalu pieces with it.
4. Boil vinegar separately. Cool it and add to the pickle. Fill into a jar.
5. Keep pickle in the sun for 5-6 days.

Amm Da Achaar

1.5 kg raw mangoes (amm)
150 gm salt
50 gms red chilli powder
25 gms haldi powder
50 gms saunf (aniseeds) - dry roast lightly
50 gms methi daana (fenugreek seeds)
30 gms kalonji (onion seeds)
2 cups mustard oil

1. Wash mangoes. Wipe with a clean cloth. Cut into 1" pieces.
2. Heat the oil in a kadhai. Remove from fire and transfer to a large pan. Cool oil.
3. Add salt, red chilli powder, haldi, saunf, methi daana and kalonji to the oil.
4. Add the mango slices to the masala oil. Mix well.
5. Fill into a jar. Keep jar in the sun, shaking it once daily.
6. To preserve the pickle for a longer time, heat some more oil and cool it.
7. Pour oil in the jar of pickle to cover the mango slices.

Mutton Achaar

Meat or pork achaar can be made in this way.
Serves 5-6

500 gms mutton (preferably boneless and without much fat)
1 tsp salt
2 cups mustard oil
2 large onions - grated or minced (chopped very finely)
6 tbsp ginger paste
2 tbsp garlic paste
2 tsp haldi powder
3 tsp red chilli powder
2 tsp salt
8 dry, red chillies
6 tsp sugar
1-1¼ cups vinegar

GRIND TOGETHER
2 tbsp rai (mustard seeds)
2 tsp kalonji (onion seeds)
4 tsp saboot dhania (coriander seeds)
2 tsp jeera (cumin seeds)

1. In a pressure cooker add washed meat, 1 tsp salt and 1 cup water. Give 3 whistles. (Mutton should get soft. The cooking time will depend on the quality of the mutton). Pressure cook on low heat for 4-5 minutes after the whistles if required.
2. When pressure drops, open the cooker and remove mutton pieces. Keep stock aside.
3. In a kadhai heat oil to smoking point. Cool.
4. Heat oil again and add onion. Fry till golden brown.
5. Add ginger and garlic paste. Fry for 1-2 minutes on low heat. Add a little stock. Fry. Go on adding some stock and frying till all the stock is used and oil floats on top.
6. Add meat, haldi, red chilli, salt, whole red chillies and sugar.
7. Add the spices ground together - rai, kalonji, dhania and jeera. Keep frying till oil floats on top.
8. Lower heat. Add 1 cup vinegar, taste and then add more if desired. Cover, lower heat and cook for 3-4 minutes or till oil floats on top, stirring occasionally.
9. Cool. Keep in a sterilized air tight container.

DRINKS

Poodina Jeera Paani

Serves 4

**4 cups water
1 rounded tbsp seedless tamarind
4 tsp lemon juice
1 tbsp sugar
½ tsp kala namak (black salt)
1½ tsp bhuna jeera (roasted cumin powder)
3/4 tsp salt, or to taste
1 bunch of mint leaves & 1" piece ginger - ground to a paste
2 tbsp besan ki pakories or boondi (raete waali pakories)**

1. Soak tamarind in 1 cup hot water. Extract pulp. Strain the pulp.
2. Grind poodina and ginger with a little water to a smooth paste.
3. Add poodina paste to tamarind water.
4. Add 3 more cups of water and all ingredients except pakories. Chill in the fridge.
5. To serve, pour in glasses and sprinkle some pakories on top.

Sardai

Serves 2-3

**250 ml (1¼ cups) milk, 250 ml (1¼ cups) water
5 tbsp sugar, or to taste**

**GRIND TOGETHER
10-15 almonds - soaked and peeled (blanched)
1½ tbsp khus khus (poppy seeds), 2 tsp magaz (water melon seeds)
10 saboot kali mirch (peppercorns)
seeds of 2 chhoti illaichi (green cardamoms)**

1. Soak khus khus, magaz, kali mirch and chhoti illaichi for 30 minutes in some water.
2. Drain and grind the khus mixture along with the blanched almonds to a very fine paste, using a little water.
3. Add ½ cup water to the almond paste. Mix. Strain and squeeze well through a muslin cloth.
4. Add remaining (3/4 cup) water and milk. Mix in the sugar. Serve chilled.

Punjabi Kanji

Red purple drink - The wine of Punjab!

Serves 12

½ kg fresh black carrots - peeled and cut into thin fingers
3 fully heaped tsp of rai powder
3 heaped tsp of salt, 2 pinches red chilli powder
½ tsp kala namak (black salt)

1. Boil 2 litres (8 cups, almost a patila full) water. When the water boils remove pan from fire.
2. Add the carrots. Let them be in hot water for 4-5 minutes.
3. Add 2 more litres (8 cups) of water & keep aside to cool. Let the water cool completely.
4. Add rai powder, salt, red chilli powder and kala namak. Mix well.
5. Transfer to an earthern or ceramic jar and keep in the sun for 2-3 days. Stir it every day.
6. After 2-3 days when it turns sour, it can be kept in the refrigerator and used as required. It is served chilled along with a few pieces of carrots.

Note:

1. Rai powder should be added only after the water turns cold.
2. If black carrots are not available, ordinary carrots and 1 beetroot may be used for colour.

Lassi - Malai Maar Ke

Serves 1

1 cup curd prepared from full cream buffalo milk
6-8 poodina (mint) leaves
½ cup water, salt and pepper to taste
½ tsp bhuna jeera powder (roasted & ground cumin seeds)

1. Beat or churn curd alongwith poodina very well, preferably in a mixi.
2. Add water, salt and pepper. Add ice and blend till frothy. Pour in a tall glass.
3. Sprinkle bhuna jeera powder and serve garnished with mint leaves.

Note: To prepare sweet lassi, add 2 tbsp sugar or gur (jaggery) to the churned curd instead of salt and pepper.

MITHA

Suji Halwa

This is made at all happy occasions in Punjabi homes.

Serves 6-8

1 cup suji/rawa, 1 cup malai/top of the milk
1 cup sugar
3-4 chhoti illaichi (green cardamoms) - powdered
½-3/4 cup chopped mixed nuts (kishmish, cashewnuts, blanched & peeled almonds)
10 tbsp pure ghee

1. Mix suji and malai well and keep aside for atleast one hour.
2. Mix sugar and 3½ cups of water. Heat and mix till sugar dissolves. Keep aside.
3. In a kadhai heat ghee. Add suji and malai mixture and fry till suji is light brown and a nice aroma is given out.
4. Add sugar and water mixture. Mix well so that no lumps remain.
5. Cook, stirring all the time till ghee separates out. Remove from heat.
6. Add illaichi powder and chopped nuts. Mix well and serve hot.

Pinni

These are made in all Punjabi households during winter months.

Serves 5-6

2 cups atta (wheat flour), 1 cup pure ghee
2 cups khoya (mawa) - crumbled
2 cups powdered sugar
3/4 cup chopped mixed nuts - kishmish (raisins), almonds etc.

1. Heat ghee in a kadhai. Reduce heat. Add atta and roast it. Keep stirring till it attains a light brown colour and a nice aroma is given out. Remove from fire.
2. In another kadhai dry roast the khoya stirring all the time till it becomes light brown.
3. Mix together roasted atta, roasted khoya, powdered sugar and nuts. Mix well.
4. Shape into round balls while still warm.

Note:

1. A little gum, deep fried and powdered can be added to the pinnis particularly when they are made for a woman who has just delivered.
2. It can be kept as it is and not shaped into balls. It is then called panjiri.

Mithae Jauley

A very popular Punjabi dessert. Is made on all happy occasions.

Serves 8-10

250 gms roasted Jauley (small, thick, vermicelli)
6 tbsp pure ghee
1 cup sugar
3 cups water
½-1 cup mixed chopped dry fruit (cashewnuts, kishmish, almonds etc.)

1. In a kadhai heat ghee. Add seviyaan (vermicelli) and fry to a rich brown colour. Do not over brown.
2. Mix sugar and water together in a separate pan. Give one boil and mix till all the sugar dissolves. Remove from fire.
3. Add sugar syrup to the seviyaan in the kadhai and boil.
4. Add dry fruit. Cover and cook till they turn soft and dry.
5. Serve hot with rabri or cold thick rice kheer or just by themselves.

Note: If using long, thin seviyaan, break the seviyaan into 3"-4" pieces. Do not cover while cooking these.

Badaam Te Gur De Laddu

Serves 6

1 cup gur ki shakkar or powdered gur
1 tbsp pure ghee
½ cup badaam (almonds) - blended roughly or finely chopped
¼ tsp ajwain

1. Heat ghee in a heavy bottomed kadhai. Add gur to it and stir, cook for a minute stirring.
2. Add ajwain and stir in almonds.
3. Remove from fire. Let it cool slightly.
4. Make marble sized balls of the prepared mixture and serve.

Note: These can be stored. It is a winter delicacy.

Chhuare Te Chaawal Di Kheer

Serves 6

1 kg full cream milk
2 chhuare (dried dates) - soaked overnight or for at least ½ hour in warm water & chopped finely
¼ cup uncooked rice - soaked for ½ hour
¼ cup sugar
a few almonds - blanched, to garnish
3-4 chhoti illaichi (green cardamoms) - powdered

1. Boil milk in a heavy bottomed kadhai. Drain rice and add to the boiling milk. Add the finely chopped chhuaras also.
2. Cook on low medium flame for 35-40 minutes, stirring frequently, till the rice is well cooked and blends well with the milk. Keep mashing the rice grains and the chhuaras also, in between. Keep scraping the sides of the kadhai too. Remove from fire when thick.
3. Add sugar and illaichi powder. Mix and transfer to a serving dish.
4. Garnish with chopped almonds. Serve hot or cold.

Pista Kesar Kulfi

Serves 6 *Picture on page 127*

1 kg (4 cups) full cream milk, a few strands of kesar (saffron)
¼ cup sugar, 2 tbsp cornflour
75 gms fresh khoya - grated & mashed slightly (3/4 cup grated)
1 tbsp pista - very finely cut
1 tbsp almonds - very finely cut
3-4 crushed chhoti illaichi (green cardamoms)

1. Dissolve cornflour in 1 cup milk and keep aside.
2. Boil the rest of the milk with kesar in a kadhai till it is reduced to half in quantity, for about 25-30 minutes on medium fire, scraping the sides.
3. Add sugar and cornflour paste. Boil. Cook for 2-3 minutes more till the sugar is well dissolved.
4. Remove from fire. Cool slightly.
5. Add khoya, almonds, pista and crushed illaichi.
6. Fill the mixture in the kulfi moulds. Freeze for 6-8 hours or overnight.

Jalebi Te Rabri

Serves 8

JALEBI
1 cup maida, 1 tbsp besan, ¼ tsp (level) soda bicarb
½ tbsp oil
½ cup thick curd
3/4 cup warm water
oil or ghee for frying

SYRUP
1¼ cups sugar, 3/4 cup water
2-3 pinches orange-red colour

1. Sieve maida, besan and soda. Add curd and oil. Add enough warm water (about 3/4 cup) to make a batter of a soft dropping consistency.
2. Beat batter well till smooth. Cover and keep aside for 30-40 minutes.
3. Heat oil or ghee in a frying pan till medium hot. Put the batter in a piping bag and make circles within circle, starting from the outside.
4. Reduce heat. Fry them golden brown on low heat on both sides, turning carefully with a pair of tongs (chimta). Remove from oil, drain excess oil and keep aside.
5. For the syrup, boil sugar, water and colour in a kadhai. After the first boil keep on low flame for 5-7 minutes till a stringy syrup is attained.
6. At serving time, dip 4-5 jalebis at a time in the hot syrup for 1 minute, take out and serve them hot with rabri.

RABRI
4 cups full cream milk
75 gm khoya - grated, (½ cup)
2 tbsp sugar
6-8 pistas - chopped
3 chhoti illaichi (green cardamoms) - powdered
rose petals or silver sheet (varq)

1. Boil milk in a heavy bottomed kadhai. Add khoya and sugar.
2. Simmer on low-medium heat for about 40-45 minutes, scraping the sides, till the quantity is reduced to almost half and the mixture turns thick with a thick pouring consistency. Remove from fire. The rabri turns thick on keeping.
3. Add some chopped pistas and cardamom powdered into the mixture.
4. Transfer to a serving dish and garnish with pistas and rose petals.
5. Chill and serve plain by itself or with jalebis or with some fruit.

Phirni

Serves 6 *Picture on page 117*

3½ cups (700 gm) milk
¼ cup basmati rice
¼ cup sugar plus 1 tbsp more, or to taste
4 almonds (badaam) - shredded, 5-6 green pistas (pistachio) - shredded
2 small silver leaves, optional
2-3 chhoti illaichi (green cardamom) - powdered
1 drop kewra essence or 1 tsp ruh kewra
a few rose petals - to decorate

1. Soak rice of good quality for about an hour in a little water.
2. Drain rice and grind with 4-5 tbsp of water to a very fine and smooth paste. Mix the rice paste with ½ cup milk and make it thinner. Keep aside.
3. Mix the rice paste with all the milk in a clean, heavy bottomed pan. Cook on medium heat, stirring continuously and let it boil. Boil, stirring constantly for 2-3 minutes more to get a mixture of creamy consistency.
4. Add sugar and cardamom powder and mix well for a few seconds.
5. Remove from fire and add ruh kewra or the essence and half of the shredded almonds and pistachios.
6. Pour the mixture into 6 small silver or earthen bowls.
7. Chill. Decorate each bowl with a silver leaf and a few shredded nuts and rose petals.

Kesar waale Mitthe Chaawal

Serves 4

1 cup Basmati rice - must be soaked for 1 hour
a few strands of kesar (saffron)
1 cup sugar
3 tbsp desi ghee
4 chhoti illaichi (green cardamoms)
3 laung (cloves)
a small piece of fresh or dried coconut - cut into thin pieces, optional
1 tbsp kishmish (raisins) - soaked in water
6-8 badam (almonds) - blanched & shredded

1. Mix 3/4 cup water and 1 cup sugar in a small pan. Add kesar. Keep on fire to boil. Stir in between. Remove from fire as soon as syrup boils. Keep aside.
2. Heat ghee in a big heavy bottomed pan. Reduce heat. Add chhoti illaichi and laung. Stir fry for a few seconds till illaichi changes colour.
3. Add coconut, almonds and kishmish. Stir till kishmish swells.
4. Discard water and add rice. Mix gently so that the rice grains do not break.
5. Add 1¼ cups water. Boil.
6. Reduce flame. Keep a tawa under the pan of rice as soon as it starts to boil to reduce the heat further.
7. Cook for about 10 minutes till the water gets absorbed.
8. Add the kesar waala sugar syrup. Mix lightly with a fork. Cover and cook further on low heat till rice is done and the syrup gets absorbed.

Pista Kesar Kulfi: Recipe on page 123 ▷

Nita Mehta's BEST SELLERS

 Cakes & Chocolates
 ZERO OIL
 ICE CREAM
 DINNER MENUS from around the world
 Food for Children
 LOW CALORIE Recipes
 LOW FAT Tasty Recipes
 Mocktails & Snacks
 PRESSURE COOKING
 Soups Salads & Starters
 SOUTH INDIAN
 The Art of BAKING
 MORE SNACKS
 Favourite NON-VEGETARIAN
 CHAAWAL
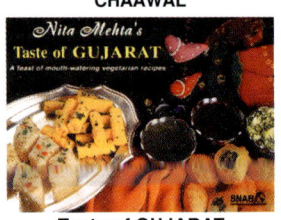 BREAKFAST NON-VEG.
 PASTA & CORN
 Taste of KASHMIR
 Taste of GUJARAT
 Taste of RAJASTHAN
 NAVRATRI RECIPES
 Green Vegetables
 PANEER All The Way
 MORE PANEER
 JHATPAT KHAANA
DESSERTS & PUDDINGS
MORE DESSERTS
Dal & Roti